The Economic and Political Consequences

of Multinational Enterprise

The Economic and Political Consequences of Multinational Enterprise:

An Anthology

RAYMOND VERNON

Herbert F. Johnson Professor of
International Business Management
Harvard University

DIVISION OF RESEARCH
GRADUATE SCHOOL OF BUSINESS ADMINISTRATION
HARVARD UNIVERSITY

Boston · 1972

Library of Congress Catalog Card No. 72–79081
ISBN 0–87584–098–1

Faculty research at the Harvard Business School is undertaken with the expectation of publication. In such publication the Faculty member responsible for the research project is also responsible for statements of fact, opinions, and conclusions expressed. Neither the Harvard Business School, its Faculty as a whole, nor the President and Fellows of Harvard College reach conclusions or make recommendations as results of Faculty research.

PRINTED IN THE UNITED STATES OF AMERICA

Table of Contents

Introduction

When an author decides to write for publication, the decision generally arises out of two convictions: that he has something to say; and that he is the one to say it. When an author arranges to republish a series of articles already in existence, it implies still another conviction: that the articles deserve to be echoed once again in the public print.

In this case, however, the decision to have the Division of Research of the Harvard Business School republish some of my articles on the multinational enterprise was based on other considerations. One of these was my desire to find ways of emphasizing the relation of the School to my studies in this field. The School's role has been critical in the creation of the materials on which this volume was based. The work itself has been a group effort at the School involving a number of my colleagues and graduate students over a period of five or six years. Even when I held the pen, they often supplied the thoughts.

A second reason for developing the anthology has to do with the media in which the articles themselves originally appeared. Those who are interested in one aspect or another of the multinational enterprise constitute a remarkably diverse and diffuse audience, difficult to reach. They include economists, political scientists, sociologists, businessmen and government officials, spread all over the globe. As a result, the publications that have come out of the School's multinational enterprise project have appeared in all sorts of highly specialized media. One paper has appeared only in an Indian publication, another in a specialized British series. The anthology, therefore, is intended to help those who follow the work of the Harvard Business School to have easier access to some of the publications.

Though endless reams have been published on the subject of the multinational enterprises over the past three or four years, we are only beginning to understand the implications of the growth of these organizations. Both the methods and the consequences of the operation of such enterprises are changing rapidly. Besides, the half-decade of research that is reflected in these pages and elsewhere is based mainly on enterprises whose parents were located in the United States. Fortunately, researchers are now beginning to develop a lively interest in the European-based and Japanese-based counterparts of the American giants. At the Harvard Business School, a major research commitment has been made to pursue that interest. The present anthology, therefore, can be thought of as an early installment in a series that will continue over the years.

RAYMOND VERNON
Herbert F. Johnson Professor
of International Business Management

Harvard Business School
Soldiers Field
Boston, Massachusetts
March 1972

Economic Sovereignty at Bay

(Reprinted from *Foreign Affairs*, October 1968,
by permission of the Council on Foreign Relations, Inc.)

Economic Sovereignty at Bay

I

Thirty-six years ago [1932], the President of the United States observed that the U.S. tariff was "solely a domestic question," a subject inappropriate for international bargaining. This view, archaic as it now may seem, stirred no public outcry, no editorial protest in the nation's leading dailies.

But that was another era.

Today, the commitments among the principal noncommunist countries of the world cover the subject of tariffs, import and export licenses, and subsidies; the level of foreign exchange rates and the price of gold; the price and quality of international air service; the price of coffee, wheat, sugar and tin; safety-at-sea standards, deep-sea fishing and whaling rights; and the international use of the ether waves. There is a pooling of foreign-aid funds through the World Bank and various regional banking institutions; a pooling of international technical assistance efforts through numerous U.N. agencies. More important still, through institutions such as the International Monetary Fund and the Organization for Economic Cooperation and Development (OECD), there are well-entrenched habits of international consultation and international persuasion on "domestic" subjects of the most sensitive sort: on internal interest rates, on budgetary and fiscal policy, and on employment and income policy. And within the European Economic Community and the European Free Trade Association both the commitments and the consultations go deeper still. A decent respect for the opinions of mankind now seems to require a willingness on the part of sovereigns to expose many critical national economic policies to the collective scrutiny of a jury of peers.

To be sure, the millennium is still far distant. Nations still take it for granted that "the vital interests" of any sovereign, as the sovereign perceives them, will take precedence over any international obligation. The 50 or 60 new countries that have erupted out of their colonial status into national independence over the past 20 years especially treasure their sovereign rights to independent action. Still, as far as the advanced countries are concerned, the generalization holds: the pattern of coordination, consultation, and commitment has evolved to such a point that freedom of economic action on the part of those nations is materially qualified.

How far will this trend go? As one looks back at the history of international economic relations, there is some basis for the view that the trend has been with us for a long time, pushed almost inexorably by advances in the technology of transport and communication, from the ocean-going windjammer to the airborne jet. But history suggests also that the responses of nations to the near-inexorable pressures for increased contact have been punctuated at times by subtle resistance or savage reaction, enough to throw the process back on its heels for protracted periods. All the elements of both the integrative process and the resistant counter-reaction are present today.

II

The persistence of man in reaching out beyond his national boundaries to exploit the economic opportunities in other lands is amply documented by history, from the Phoenicians' investments in the tin mines of Cornwall to Fiat's commitments in the Soviet Union. For many decades before World War I, international economic ties were critical to the economies that today are thought of as "advanced." Migration was high; capital was flowing across international boundaries at impressive rates; and there were considerable movements of goods among these countries.

From World War I to World War II, the technology of international transportation and communication steadily advanced. But with the characteristic perverseness that punctuates the history of human institutions, the advanced nations demonstrated that they were not the passive pawns of technological change and were quite capable of resisting the implications of such change for a decade or two. While world production went up something like 40 percent in the interwar period, nations managed to suppress the growth of world trade so that it increased by only half the production rate. International investment also was restricted; after an ebullient period of growth in the 1920s, the flow of investment was curbed and reversed in the 1930s.

In general, the interwar period was an era of early Keynesian experimentation, an interval in which many nations turned inward to learn if a proper mix of autarkic national policies could generate full employment and reasonable rates of growth. As part of the disposition for each nation to try to fend for itself, there was a rash of competitive devaluations and export subsidies, coupled with national policies aimed at propping up internal demand and floating national economies off the shoals. To implement these policies, it was necessary for governments to restrict trade and control capital movements, irrespective of the integrating pressures created by the advances in transport and communication.

The restrictive initiatives of governments between the two great wars were abetted by equally restrictive undertakings on the part of international business. By World War I, leading national firms in different countries had already begun to have painful encounters with one another in international markets. Part of the contact was by way of competition in international trade, especially for new products in the fields of chemicals, transportation, electrical equipment, and machinery. But part of the contact took place by even more intrusive means. A few scores of U.S. enterprises invested in overseas manufacturing subsidiaries, locating them in many instances within the markets of their principal international competitors; a smaller number of European firms did the same. Somehow, as many businessmen of the era saw it, the bruising contacts between business interests from different countries had to be arrested and contained. Accordingly, wherever a few large firms or a few strong producer associations controlled national industries, the industries concerned set about creating agreements that divided world markets on national lines or shared them pro rata among the producers from different nations, thereby limiting the flow of international trade and investment.

While governments and enterprises were busily attempting to clamp down the flow of international transactions, the objective conditions for the growth of those activities perversely continued to improve. World War II accelerated the trend spectacularly. It shrank the Atlantic crossing from four days to seven hours. It turned transatlantic tourism from a rich man's indulgence into a middleclass need. It opened up the possibility for international consultations on a day-to-day basis not only between the officials of governments but also between the engineers, controllers, salesmen, and strategists of private firms.

In the years immediately following World War II, before the prewar international cartels could effectively regroup, American businessmen rediscovered Europe; at the same time Europeans began to rediscover one another and the American market. This time, however, the contacts were not confined to a few hundred firms on each side of the Atlantic, but were spread over some thousands of enterprises.

The full force of the acceleration in international contacts

did not emerge, however, until the early 1960s. By that time
the improvements in transportation and communication had
been assisted by a wholesale dismantling of governmental
restrictions on trade, payments and capital movements among
the countries of the advanced world. It was then that the
magnitude of the explosion in the international exchange of
goods, money, people, and ideas really began to be evident.
From 1953 to 1965 the volume of international trade in
manufactured goods among the advanced countries almost
tripled, outrunning the expansion of production by a very
considerable margin. Symptomatic of one of the factors behind the increase was the spectacular growth in international
air freight, which rose steadily by 20 percent or so per year
(in ton-miles). The arrivals and departures of international
travelers in North America and Europe grew about 10 percent annually. And direct investment by U.S. interests in
the other advanced countries rose annually by about the
same percentage.

It was not merely the quantum jump in international contacts that mattered; it was a change in the quality of those
contacts as well. The development of a Eurodollar market
abroad is illustrative of that qualitative change. Here is a
market in which the sale of several billion dollars' worth of
paper, denominated in U.S. currency, is being transacted annually between principals who have no ties of residence or
nationality to the United States. Commercial banks throughout Europe use Eurodollars with aplomb, often for purely
local purposes. Sometimes, for instance, these instruments
are used by banks to lay off the surplus funds of their local
economies, sometimes to acquire needed funds for local
loans.

The quality of the interpenetration and interdependence
of the advanced countries is suggested by many other indices,
some quite subtle in character. Young Europeans feel de-
tached from the concept of the nation-state: "We are all

German Jews," chorused the French student militants as
they marched on the National Assembly. There is a willingness to place on the agenda of the OECD and other international organizations such sensitive domestic issues as the
monetary and fiscal policies of member governments. And
there is a proliferation of private organizations, such as the
multinational enterprises, with structures that take only casual account of the way in which sovereign states have drawn
their national boundaries.

III

The multinational enterprise provides a striking illustration of the extent to which modern means of communication
permit an integrated organization to link resources in different national economies in order to serve a common set of
organizational aims. The term "multinational enterprise"
is sometimes confusing and always imprecise; but what I
have in mind here is simply a cluster of corporations of diverse nationality joined together by ties of common ownership and responsive to a common management strategy.
That kind of definition serves well enough to characterize
Ford or Nestlé, IBM or Philips.

Nothing is altogether without precedent in human insti-
tution-building; but the multinational enterprise, as I use
the term here, comes very close to lacking a relevant precedent.

It was not until the latter part of the nineteenth century
that nations began to allow businessmen, as a routine matter
of right, to create corporations without limit of life or size
of function. And it has only been six or seven decades since
most jurisdictions permitted corporations to own other corporations. Because businessmen were not slow to exercise
their new prerogatives, it rapidly became commonplace to
find clusters of corporations linked together by a common

parent, sharing a common pool of resources, and adhering to a common strategy.

Already before World War I there were a few international clusters of corporations containing entities of diverse nationalities within a common organizational structure. Two dozen oil and mining companies, several scores of manufacturing companies, and a few banks and insurance companies made up most of the list. Not all of these, however, pretended to administer their far-flung subsidiaries in accordance with a common strategy. As long as the time-cost of face-to-face consultation among corporate affiliates in different countries was so high, there was neither much need nor much opportunity to develop a tight, continuous, and integral strategy among them. Accordingly, the subsidiaries remote from the parents that had created them often fell under the effective control of local strong men.

By 1950 over 400 U.S. companies had assets of $1 million or more in foreign direct investments. But even at that late date, it is doubtful that many saw their foreign investments as much more than peripheral to the corporate structure. The domestic U.S. market was still the serious business of most of these enterprises. The requirements of that market usually determined the mix and design of the firm's products, the direction of its technological curiosity and the nature of its preferred production process. The dollar was thought of as the riskless medium of exchange, while all other currencies were thought of as involving special risk. The Americans in the enterprise were the "natives" of the microcosm, while others in the enterprise were the "foreigners."

In the late 1950s there were major signs of change, and in the ten years that followed the change went very deep. Two tendencies in particular became evident. One strong tendency, especially apparent in the corporate clusters headed by U.S. parents, was toward the reorganization of the control and command mechanism. The "international vice president" or his equivalent, brought into being by the first burst of overseas interest, is rapidly being eliminated. This change is not a sign of the downgrading of the organization's interest in foreign markets, but the very opposite. It is a sign of the elevation and absorption of the business done "abroad" into the mainstream of corporate strategy. In some cases it is more; it is the beginning of the obliteration of the invidious distinction inside the corporation between "home business" and "foreign business." It is the emergence of the strategic view that business should find the best markets, employ the best technology, finance through the best channels, irrespective of geography. It would be pushing history more than a little to say that the U.S. parent firms of multinational enterprises have reached the point at which their affinity to the dollar is no greater than to the franc, or that their identification with Italian markets is as close as with American, or even that their executive recruiting system is as partial to Bavarians as to Hoosiers. But that is the direction of the movement.

The second visible tendency in the structure of U.S. parent firms, closely related to the first, has been the in-gathering of foreign subsidiaries, wherever they may be, under the discipline and framework of a common global strategy and a common global control. The headquarters planning of many of these enterprises is more "global" today than it has ever been. It is capable of scanning the world for sales opportunities or production sites or capital supplies or technical skills with greater ease and sophistication than ten years ago. International procurement, crosshauling and distribution are becoming a commonplace.

One ought not draw the inference from this description that the corporate officers of the subsidiaries are mere puppets of the center, yanked about by computers operating from a distant common post. Many have the discretion to tailor the commands from the center to their local needs.

But their conditioning and their objectives are designed to contribute to a common organizational strategy of some sort; otherwise there would be no reason for the existence of the multinational enterprise.

In appraising the possibilities of a reaction to the trend, one has to be aware that the nation-state has sometimes felt threatened by the trend in rather sensitive areas of its existence. So far, multinational enterprises have been concentrated largely in a few industries — in oil and mining, drugs and chemicals, machinery, transportation equipment, and food and tobacco. A few of these industries, as it happens, embrace national activities in which nation-states feel a special vulnerability and insecurity; some of these industries, for instance, relate to the national defense or to irreplaceable national resources or to technological leadership.

To add to the tension, nation-states have come to give credence to some of the more uninhibited projections of the future which picture the multinational enterprise as the overwhelmingly dominant vehicle of the world's business. This kind of projection, one ought to note, is not based on very solid evidence. On the contrary, various studies indicate that with every passing decade, as the world's markets grow, the basic standardized industries, such as aluminum, steel and oil, contain a growing number of firms, not a declining number. More generally, as the technology of any line becomes well and widely known and as the markets for an established product enlarge, additional producers find the barriers to entry less formidable and manage to gain a foothold. It is not foreordained, therefore, that mankind will be swallowed up by the International Colossus Corporation. Nonetheless, that fear exists.

Still another source of the tension created by multinational enterprises arises out of the fact that about four out of five such enterprises are headed by U.S. parents, and that the activity of these enterprises is usually thought of by other nations as an extension of the American hegemony. The notion that the General Motors' subsidiary in France in some sense represents an extension of U.S. economic domination to the soil of France may seem a trifle farfetched to most Americans. The interests of General Motors and those of the United States are usually carefully differentiated and sometimes sharply distinguished by the American political process. To Europeans, however, the distinction is not readily evident.

Basing their reaction on an amalgam of fact, fear, and fancy, therefore, many governments view the multinational enterprise with a sense of acute discomfort. Few governments would be able to say precisely how and when they expect the global interests of the enterprise to conflict with the national interests of the economy; many of the illustrations that are used to document the fear are patently exceptional or farfetched. But as long as the multinational enterprise has the power, difficult or improbable though its use may sometimes be, to dry up technology or export technicians or drain off capital or reduce production or shift profits or alter prices or allocate export markets, there is a latent or active tension associated with its presence. As long as they are predominantly headed by U.S. firms, there is also a fear that they may be the instruments of U.S. policy. For some governments the tension can be tolerated perfectly well, but for others the sense of loss of control has been much more difficult to abide.

IV

Although it is unlikely that the business of the advanced world will be dominated by a few large firms, it is more than probable that the economic links between the national economies of the advanced world will become even deeper and more intimate. The increasing intimacy of these ties presents challenges of a new order to the individual nation-state.

Picture the economy of any of the advanced countries of North America or Europe as I have sketched it. It is an economy that draws a considerable part of its technology from outside its boundaries, even while it exports a continuous flow of information to others; it relies upon the plants of other nations to provide a flow of critical products, while relying also upon their markets to absorb substantial proportions of the products it generates; it draws on the savings of nationals in other countries for some purposes, while exporting quantities of its own savings to satisfy the needs of others; it offers sanctuary to enterprises which frame their strategy in global terms, while expecting some of its own nationals to establish themselves in other countries in pursuit of a global strategy.

One cannot easily trace out all the consequences of this pattern of interpenetration. Some of those consequences, however, are reasonably clear. When the rediscount rate is hiked in New York, the cost of money rises in Brussels; when the United States runs a large budgetary deficit, inflationary pressures build up in Europe; more generally, when Italy has an earthquake, dishes rattle in Holland.

From the point of view of national governments, such a degree of openness on the part of national economies is disconcerting enough. Whatever happens in any economy becomes the pressing business of all the others: a general strike in France; a fall of government in Britain. Regardless of the complex political jockeying that may be going on at a moment of economic crisis, there are compelling pressures on each country to help douse the other's fires. The French disdain of British economic management before their own May [1968] fiasco did not altogether exempt them from the need to assist the pound sterling in crisis. The wry American satisfaction at de Gaulle's discomfiture did not permit the

U.S. government to disregard the need to support the franc.

The interdependence of the advanced nations has made them especially vulnerable to the consequences when one of them decides to place a block in the system. When the United States began imposing restrictions on the export of its capital, the government of Canada felt threatened. The remedy for Canada's problems was in some sense even more disconcerting for the nation-state concept than the original threat had been; in order to continue receiving the necessary flow of capital from the United States, Canada undertook to restrain the reexport of capital to third countries.

Those same United States restrictions led to largely unanticipated consequences for European capital markets. The subsidiaries of U.S. enterprises, eager to continue building their European business, searched the European economies for idle cash with which to finance their expansion. To help them in the search, American investment bankers made complex partnerships with European financial interests. Coupling American mass selling expertise with European savoir faire, these transatlantic syndicates sold some billions of dollars of bonds on the European market, thus changing rather dramatically both the channels and the instruments to which European savings were being drawn.

There is still another implication of the close ties among the economies of the advanced nations, one which in the end may prove the most disconcerting of all. A considerable part of the international flow of money, goods, and services among these economies can no longer be thought of as arm's-length transactions. Many of these transactions take place between the sister affiliates of multinational entities. For instance, close to one-third of U.S. exports of nonmilitary manufactured goods, about $6 billion annually, is shipped to the overseas affiliates of U.S. parent firms, while over $5 billion are returned annually to the United States by such affiliates in the form of dividends, interest, and royalties.

Apart from the international transactions that take place under the mantle of multinational enterprise, there are also the transactions that take place among the members of more informal international alliances. For instance, the commercial banking and investment banking systems of the advanced countries are now so intimately intertwined that it would be distorting reality to think of many of their transactions as representing arm's-length exchanges.

When international transactions are effected between parties whose relationships are long-term and organic in character, the regulatory capabilities of an intervening state inevitably decline. As a result, any state which senses an inadequacy in its capacity to impose effective restrictions at the border has ample reason for harboring that feeling. For brief periods of time, perhaps, regulatory controls may have a real impact; for longer periods, the illusion of such impact may persist simply because the specific channel that had been blocked by a particular set of controls was responding in line with governmental expectations. But given the complexity of multinational institutions and the presence of so many alternative channels for the legitimate international movement of funds and other resources, the regulating sovereign seems increasingly at a disadvantage.

V

The advanced world, carried ebulliently on the crest of a technological revolution in transportation and communication, has absentmindedly set up a virile system of international institutions and relationships that sit alongside the system of nation-states. The system of nation-states has its built-in machinery of political process and public accountability, while the international system wields its power and garners its support by less well-defined means.

In part, the two systems are complementary; in part they

are at odds. The international system, when operating benignly, stands for all the good things that can be achieved by open boundaries: more trade, more capital flows, more movement of ideas and people, more growth. The system of nation-states, at its best, stands for all the good things that national policy can hope to provide: more economic security, more social equality, more identification and a sense of belonging. An economic determinist, if asked to project the outcome of the clash between the systems, would probably lean toward the assumption that the international order will prevail. The shrinkage of international distances will continue; the flow of international ideas will accelerate; the opportunities and the requirements of large-scale human endeavor will increase.

But such a prediction, if it were made, would be far too facile, especially for the three or four decades ahead that represent the planning horizon of most of us. There is a stubborn life and purpose in the system of nation-states, and there is a tenacious capacity on the part of mankind indefinitely to disregard the seemingly inevitable. It is perfectly possible, therefore, to picture a sequence of events in which the increasing openness of national boundaries leads to a reaction of disconcerting force. Restrictions on the flow of capital, goods, and people could conceivably be the first response to the difficulties and uncertainties that have been generated by the relatively open boundaries of the past decade or two. In classic Hegelian fashion the world may experience a period of revulsion from the international order before it is prepared to move on to a new international synthesis.

Some kinds of problems are less likely to touch off a spasm of revulsion and withdrawal than are others. I would worry only a little, for instance, about the problems that arise over the conflicting jurisdictional reach of nation-states, such as the efforts of one nation to influence the actions of the nationals of another. Conflicts of this sort, which appear from time to time in fields such as antitrust or trading with the enemy or securities regulation, can be handled reasonably well as nations grow more sensitive to the problem. A tolerable state of affairs can be created partly by the nation-states' application of self-imposed constraints and partly by their negotiation of common standards.

There are some problems, however, whose solution is not amenable to modest measures of that sort. Some demand consciously coordinated action among sovereigns on issues that are fairly sensitive in terms of domestic politics. The balance-of-payments issue, for instance, when it involves agreements among governments to create Special Drawing Rights (SDRs) or "paper gold," begins to move into sensitive territory. The existence of agreements of this sort may go unnoticed by the politicians for a period of time, provided they are sufficiently technical and obscure. But when they begin to demand coordinated economic action tending to restrict the freedom of states to frame independent domestic policies, one can expect to see the beginnings of major difficulty. When this interrelation becomes widely apparent, co-ordinated action may be resisted by all the principal actors involved: by the governments which would have to share their power with others; and by the enterprises whose transactions would be the subject of the coordinated governmental control.

If governments were obliged to coordinate their monetary, fiscal, and other economic policies on any intimate and continuous basis, the consequences would presumably affect all business, whether oriented to the domestic market or to the international market. But multinational enterprises would have an especially heavy stake in such a trend. In some respects, the trend could increase the freedom of multinational enterprises; but the opposite may also be true. Intergovernmental coordination might, for instance, reduce the number of situations in which the rights afforded by some governments were thwarted by the regulations imposed by others. On the other hand, since there are some things that governments can do together which they cannot do separately, intergovernmental coordination could have the effect of increasing the effectiveness of regulations by the public sector in many fields, including taxation and monetary regulation.

In general, multinational enterprises as a group have exhibited no great enthusiasm for a coordinated approach by sovereign states to the problems that the states addressed individually in the past. Such a reserved reaction is readily understandable. The largest and most seasoned of such enterprises can point with justifiable pride to the fact that, despite the pitfalls and dangers that uncoordinated sovereign action may theoretically offer to multinational enterprises, few of them have fallen victim to the dangers of six or seven decades of war, depression, and tension. As far as such enterprises are concerned, a heavy presumption exists that they would continue to survive even in an uncoordinated world.

Instead of subjecting themselves to the uncertain consequences of multinational coordination, most such enterprises are quite ready to commit themselves to a "code of good behavior" toward the economies in which their affiliates are established. These enterprises are aware that their "conduct" has generally been quite reasonable and acceptable when viewed by any normal standards. Accordingly, most of them have been willing to commit themselves on paper to the continuation of such conduct. They are usually prepared to agree to train local nationals, observe local customs, obey local laws, and perform all the other acts expected of decent local citizens. But "conduct" — at least "conduct" defined in these terms — is not very relevant to the underlying issue. With varying degrees of intensity, nation-states have a sense that the locus of their power is challenged by an open international system in general and by multinational enterprises in particular. What some are searching for is the means of checking their sense of ebbing control and of retaining a tolerable amount of that power.

It may be that, in the end, sovereign states will learn to live with a decline in their perceived economic power. But one marvels at the tenacity with which man seeks to retain a sense of differentiation and identity, a feeling of control, even when the apparent cost of the identity and the control seems out of all proportion to its value. One cannot disregard the possibility that one of the advanced countries, imperiled by a sense of ebbing control and declining identity, may strike out blindly against the others.

The role of statesmen in a situation of this kind is to find the means for accommodating the tension before it grows intolerable. In this case the accommodation will be painful and complex. On the part of governments, it will involve agreements that demand the conscious sharing of prerogatives that once were independently exercised. On the part of business, it may demand a tolerance for more coordinated and more effective measures of public control. Whether the advanced world has the resiliency and farsightedness to take the needed steps remains an open question.

Foreign Trade and Foreign Investment: Hard Choices for Developing Countries

(Reprinted from *Foreign Trade Review*, January–March 1971,
by permission of *Foreign Trade Review*,
Indian Institute of Foreign Trade, New Delhi)

Foreign Trade and Foreign Investment: Hard Choices for Developing Countries

Those who must wrestle from day to day with the problems of India's development surely feel overwhelmed at times by what has yet to be achieved. Those, such as myself, who can afford the luxury of surveying India's record from a long-run point of view are impressed as much by the accomplishments as by the remaining problems. Not the least of these accomplishments is the development of a modern industrial sector in India capable of supplying a considerable part of India's industrial needs and of exporting some of its output to the rest of the world.

India's modern industrial growth has been based partly upon its own resources and partly upon resources from abroad. The industrial techniques that are embodied in the plant and the machinery of India's industrial sector come mainly from the more advanced countries. But the investment and the manpower that have put the technology to work in the Indian economy are mainly national in origin. In India's case, the limited contribution of foreigners to both investment and manpower is no accident. India's national policies have on the whole tended to be relatively restrictive toward foreign direct investors, laying down conditions for entry and conditions for subsequent operation that strongly limit the foreigners' perceptions of opportunities for growth and profit.

Any nation that has thought very much about its policy toward foreign direct investment, as India clearly has, generally finds itself juggling with three sets of objectives. One of these is the desire for rapid growth. A second is the desire for the achievement of an equitable distribution of income, both among the various classes that are affected by the industrialization process and among the various regions of the country that are competing for the nation's scarce resources. A third objective is to control one's own national destiny, to the extent that the conditions of world society permit. It is not for outsiders such as myself to suggest how important each of these objectives may be, especially when the objectives conflict with one another. The kind of choice that is needed in cases of that sort is for the country itself to make. Still, an outsider's view can sometimes contribute a little to the process of choice by reintroducing familiar facts from a different point of view.

Performance of Foreign Direct Investors [1]

For the past decade or two, scholars have had the opportunity to examine fairly closely the operations of large multinational enterprises, as they have established manufacturing subsidiaries in the economies of less developed countries throughout the world. As a result, it is possible to sort out more clearly just what takes place in the course of such operations. Some firmly held preconceptions, it appears, require amending.

It may be that in an earlier and simpler era, capital transfers were the most important economic aspect of foreign direct investment; but that situation, if it ever existed, has

[1] The conclusions in this section have been presented at much greater length in a book published by Basic Books (New York, 1971, *Sovereignty at Bay: The Multinational Spread of U.S. Enterprises*). Research, on which the book is based, was financed by The Ford Foundation.

long since passed. When a foreign enterprise sets up a subsidiary in a less developed country today, the principal consequence is to link a business entity inside the country with a multinational mechanism. A mechanism of this sort has a capacity to mobilize the money, men, and methods necessary for the production and sale of goods. The resources employed by the multinational mechanism need not be its own. The subsidiary's capital, in the typical case, comes mainly from sources other than the parent. For instance, in recent years the subsidiaries of U.S. parents in less developed countries have drawn three or four times as much capital from non-U.S. capital sources as from U.S. sources in connection with the financing of their operations. The multinational enterprise also has a well-developed capacity, as a rule, for locating critically needed information that lies outside its structure, such as information of a technological nature or information on the characteristics of markets. Economists have gradually come to realize that the capacity to mobilize information of this sort may be no less valuable than capital in its more traditional forms, and may be even more difficult for the developing country to acquire. This is one reason why so much emphasis is being placed of late upon the subject of "human capital" as distinguished from capital in its more conventional forms.

Recent studies have indicated more clearly not only what the multinational enterprise has to offer but also what circumstances are most likely to generate the offer. The interest of multinational enterprises in establishing manufacturing subsidiaries in less developed countries is being recognized as a phenomenon that in some respects is regular and predictable.

In the decade following World War II, the interest that most multinational enterprises displayed for countries like India was primarily as a potential market, not as a site for production. Such enterprises had their production facilities already established in the United States, Europe, or Japan. The less developed world, as seen through their eyes, presented all of the complexities and uncertainties that go with newly established political independence. Accordingly, there was little reason to give serious thought to the possibility of establishing production facilities inside such areas.

Here and there, however, an enterprise or two could see some advantages in setting up local processing facilities. Some of these exceptional cases were a carryover from an era of greater political security, such as the pre-Independence period. Other cases were stimulated by the opportunity to reduce transportation costs associated with the shipment of goods from far-off places. Accordingly, one saw the development of automobile assembly plants, pharmaceuticals packaging plants, and the like, as convenient adjuncts for serving local markets.

Nations with large internal markets had a major bargaining counter for persuading the foreign investor to take the next step; and some of those countries used that counter skillfully and well. These countries commonly selected industries that they thought might be established on their own soil, then imposed heavy import restrictions on the products of these industries from abroad. At that juncture, the foreign manufacturers that had been serving local markets were confronted with the question whether to invest in production facilities inside the market. Some preferred not to; but many more pursued that possibility very actively.

Some countries, confronted with an interest on the part of foreign enterprises to establish local manufacturing facilities, were content to authorize such investment without extensive conditions of any sort. Other countries, however, have preferred to lay down a rather extensive network of conditions, aimed at insuring that foreign profits were not exorbitant, that foreign management personnel did not dominate the subsidiary, that the balance-of-payments impact

on the operation was favorable, and so on. The immediate effect of restrictions of this sort has been, inevitably, that the volume of foreign direct investment has been a little lower than it otherwise would have been. Whether that consequence is "good" or "bad," however, depends upon some extraordinarily complex judgments to which this paper will shortly return.

In any case, the foreign-owned manufacturing subsidiaries that established themselves inside the large less developed countries, as a rule, were concerned first of all with serving local markets. Up to 1965 or so, the principal activity of such enterprises consisted of becoming acclimated to the risks and opportunities that the new environment afforded, adapting their operations to the local costs and local factor availabilities, and building up their levels of production for the local market.

Some four or five years ago, however, a new trend became apparent. Some multinational enterprises appeared to be learning how to use their subsidiaries in the less developed areas as part of an international logistical system. The productive facilities of such enterprises were being integrated into a very much larger global framework. The huge international automobile enterprises were found manufacturing parts that were destined for export to assembly plants in other countries. The large multinational electronics firms were engaged in similar pursuits. Some enterprises that produced broad lines of consumer appliances, such as sewing machines and stoves, were found producing the simpler and less expensive models in plants located in developing areas to be shipped to markets located all over the world.

For a time, it was fashionable for observers to think cases of this sort as trivial and idiosyncratic. By 1970, however, enough information had been developed to indicate that the propensity for foreign-owned subsidiaries in the developing countries to export a portion of their output had grown

into a phenomenon of rather considerable significance. In Latin America, for instance, annual exports of this sort had passed well beyond the $1 billion mark. Even in India, the importance of the phenomenon had begun to be noted.

The new trend in the use of the subsidiaries in developing countries as logistical points in an international network, has been the result of a number of different forces. One of these has simply been a natural learning process. The initial perceptions of foreign investors regarding the conditions under which they would be obliged to produce in developing countries have changed over the course of time. As investors have become familiar with the local environment, they have learned to live with its difficulties and adapt to its opportunities more effectively.

Another factor has been the sheer increase in the volume of production that has taken place in some of these foreign-owned subsidiaries. With increasing volumes, unit costs have gone down; and with declining unit costs, the possibilities for export have increased.

A third factor has been the increased efficiency of local labor and local suppliers, an efficiency that could often be traced to the training efforts of the management of foreign enterprise itself.

There has been a fourth factor still: the unremitting pressure of some government on foreign investors to generate exports, as a condition for their continuing to operate inside the local market. Pressures of that sort have sometimes altogether repelled foreign investors and led them to look elsewhere; but in other cases, when the pressures have been applied in the appropriate time and form, they have had the desired result.

As foreigners have learned more about the conditions of production in less developed countries, and as governments have learned more about the operations of multinational enterprises, some of the naiveté of earlier debates over the

merits and drawbacks of foreign direct investment has begun to diminish. In the earliest discussions, questions of profit levels and of balance-of-payments consequences often tended to dominate. A decade or more of study and discussion, however, has begun to indicate that the important questions may lie elsewhere.

Take the balance-of-payments question. How is one to determine whether foreign direct investors place an undesirable burden on the country's balance-of-payments position?

To answer that question, one has to decide what he thinks the country would have looked like if the foreign investor had not made his commitment. If the products that the foreign-owned facilities generate would otherwise not have been produced at all, then any measurement of the balance-of-payments impact of the foreign commitment has to include that salient fact. The foreign investment must not only be associated with the profit flow that its success eventually generates; it must also be credited with the savings in imports and the increase in exports that its presence generates, and must be charged with any increase in imports that its operations entail.

The few serious studies that have sought to capture these complex effects have ended up with results that tend to defuse the balance-of-payments issue and to relegate it to a lesser level of acuity. This is the case partly because such studies reveal how difficult it is to measure the balance-of-payments effect in a way that has real meaning; at the same time, such studies disclose how sensitive the results are to the assumptions — the unavoidably arbitrary assumptions — of the researcher. If it is assumed, for instance, that foreign investment accelerates the process of import substitution or export enlargement, if it is assumed that foreign enterprises use local resources more efficiently than a local entrepreneur might do, these assumptions turn out to dominate the outcome of the calculation.

On reflection, it is also clear why the question of profit levels has a smaller significance than it is generally accorded. The profits of foreign-owned manufacturing enterprises in less developed countries, taken as an average, tend to be of the order of 10 percent or so of the sales of those subsidiaries. To be sure, not all industries are found operating at the 10 percent level; some are lower and some a good deal higher. Clearly, too, profits that were smaller might be better for the host country, especially if a portion of the profits were being shipped out of the economy. But it is just as clear, given the relative magnitudes involved, that assumptions about the remaining 90 percent of output could have powerful consequences in determining whether the investment as a whole was being productive or contra productive from the viewpoint of the developing country. In the extreme case, if the 90 percent would not have been produced at all, the fact would overwhelm the final judgment; or if produced with a lower efficiency, that fact could also be of great importance in balance-of-payments terms. In short, enterprises with "low" profits can easily be less useful to the nation than those with "high."

From the viewpoint of the government regulator concerned to ensure that the local economy was deriving maximum benefit from the foreign investment, these studies indicate the gross inadequacies of conventional measures of performance. Perhaps the most misleading of all is the usual "return-on-investment" measure by which the foreign investors are commonly judged. In practice, as it turns out, neither the profit that is assigned to the subsidiary nor the capital that is ascribed to it by the conventional yardsticks of the chartered accountant has much to do with assessing the economic impact of the investment itself. Subsidiary profits are unavoidably arbitrary, especially when subsidiaries are intimately linked to a multinational system; they involve an apportionment of the costs of the multinational mechanism; they require the setting of prices between affiliate companies; they entail the determination of royalties and administrative charges in order to reflect the services performed by the multinational system. And there is no way by which allocations of this sort can avoid their arbitrary qualities.

The capital that is normally ascribed to the local manufacturing subsidiary of multinational enterprises is no less arbitrary than profits that are normally assigned to that subsidiary — and in some ways a good deal more misleading. The important contribution of the multinational enterprise, if it makes any contribution at all, is the access that it provides for the subsidiary to an international network that the enterprise has created. Access to knowledge about markets, technology, and so on, is much more unique and much less dispensable than access to finance capital. This fact varies in importance according to the nature of the subsidiary operation. It is much more important with respect to subsidiaries that export their products than those which do not; much more important for enterprises engaged in complex operations than those that produce simple products by simple methods.

The more one looks at the available facts with regard to the operations of foreign-owned enterprises, the more one feels obliged to turn away from economic questions and to look for political or social factors as an explanation of the tensions associated with such enterprises. On the one hand, such countries feel the need to keep a welcome mat at the front door because of the possible economic benefits that might accrue from the presence of these enterprises; on the other, they sense that the enterprises constitute a multifaceted challenge for the local economy. The challenge involves such key elite groups as government officials, local businessmen, and intellectuals. For government officials, the challenge is often perceived as a competing bid for the economic control of the country. For local businessmen, the challenge takes the form of a threat that they may be excluded from lines of manufacturing activity to which they aspire. For intellectual groups, the challenge is more subtle and perhaps more profound; in some countries, intellectuals see the foreign investors as strengthening the hands of an Establishment against which they are pitted, while in other countries the challenge is seen as a war between conflicting ideologies.

Any realistic policy toward foreign enterprise in a developing country has to take into account all of these variables. The object of economic growth, taken by itself, cannot be expected to determine national policy. Questions of the distribution of income, power, status, and other kudos by which men live, will be just as important in the determination of national policy.

Choice of Policies

Confronted with a mix of perceived advantages and disadvantages from the operations of the foreign-owned subsidiary, many countries such as India have sought to develop a set of policies that would generate the largest advantage for them, by carefully screening all foreign proposals and by laying down conditions on their operations in the country. Some nations have been in a better position to impose conditions than have others. For instance, countries with large internal markets could demand more than those that had smaller markets; countries with stable exchange rates and favorable cost conditions were in a comparatively strong bargaining position; and, finally, countries that seemed able potentially to develop their own internal capabilities for modern production were able to impose conditions more effectively than those that did not seem to possess this attribute.

In the choice of strategy toward foreign investors, one central question has been whether to make the initial entry relatively easy and to apply conditions later; or, alternatively, whether to impose onerous conditions at the very outset. For numerous reasons, the first approach has been far more successful than the second.

The mind of a prospective foreign investor who, for the first time, is considering whether to invest in a country such as India, is inevitably assailed with a host of uncertainties and doubts. From his point of view, the venture on which he is about to embark is located in *terra incognita*. Feasibility studies, engineering studies, marketing studies and the like may reduce the sense of uncertainty somewhat; but, as any businessman of experience knows, such studies are entitled to only a limited amount of weight in assessing the difficulties that are likely to arise in actual practice.

As a result, the risk that the foreign businessman associates with an investment in a less developed country is likely to be the highest at the time of entry and to decline thereafter. Hence, the margins of safety, the guarantees, and the profit targets that the businessman is likely to look for also will be at their highest at the time of entry.

Once the initial step has been taken, however, perceptions change. For one thing, after a multinational enterprise has operated a subsidiary in a less developed country for a number of years, its investment in the learning process is behind it. That initial cost, once sunk, need not burden the operation again. The calculations of the enterprise concerning the wisdom of staying in the country, being based upon its assessment of future marginal cost against marginal benefit, will treat sunk cost as sunk. Besides, the acquisition of knowledge, more often than not, reduces the perception of risk. Accordingly, the later calculations of the foreign investor are likely to look for a lower profit target and to require fewer guarantees than the initial calculation would require. This may be why countries like Mexico and Colombia appear, on the whole, to have a greater success in their policies toward attracting the desired foreign direct investment than have India and Pakistan. Those countries have followed a policy that is less draconian than India's in demanding conditions at the outset. The subsidiaries of foreign-owned enterprises nevertheless have enlarged and deepened their functions over the course of time, sometimes with official persuasion, sometimes without. Such steps have been related to a changing perception of the nature of the risks involved in undertaking the next step in the process.

Joint Ventures

Another policy that has distinguished different countries in their approach to foreign-owned subsidiaries involves the issue of joint ventures with local interests. Many less developed countries follow a policy of requiring that some portion of the equity of foreign-owned subsidiaries should be held in local hands. But some insist more firmly than others. When confronted with determined foreign investors who are in a strong position to bargain, some governments retain enough flexibility to consider whether a wholly owned subsidiary is to be preferred to no investment at all.

It is not at all clear that such flexibility is inimical to the interests of the countries concerned. In recent years, a number of studies have shed light on the nature of the relationships between foreign parent companies and their joint ventures. These studies suggest that the purposes which less developed countries have in mind when insisting upon joint ventures are in fact only imperfectly achieved. In some cases, in fact, the interests of the developing countries, when weighed in economic terms alone, seem very badly served by joint-venture arrangements.

One result that host governments hope to achieve by insisting upon joint ventures is a less intimate, more arm's-length relationship between parent and subsidiary. Various shreds of data suggest that this objective, considered by itself, is often achieved: parents in fact do seem to deal with joint ventures on a less intimate and more formal basis than with wholly owned subsidiaries.

The implications of that statement, however, should be made very clear. Understandably, in the case of joint ventures, parents are much less disposed to transfer technology without payment or to sell intermediate products at preferential prices or to provide working funds without interest payments. The counterpart of this statement, to be sure, is that parents also feel less free, when their interests require, to draw funds away from the joint venture or to levy discriminatory prices upon the joint venture in the sale of intermediate products. On balance, therefore, the outcome of relations between parent and the joint venture are somewhat more predictable than with the wholly owned subsidiary, and more nearly approximate an arm's-length outcome; but they are not necessarily more favorable to the subsidiary. Although the evidence is not overwhelming, there are indications that in the early stages of the parent-subsidiary relationship — that is, in the stages when subsidiaries are being launched — wholly owned subsidiaries are treated more favorably than joint ventures. It could be that the opposite is the case in later stages of the parent-subsidiary relationship, but the evidence on this point is too weak for any conclusion.

Of the various studies of parent-subsidiary relationships as they are affected by joint ventures, some of the most common are studies to determine if parents impose territorial restraints upon the selling activities of the subsidiaries. Are joint ventures constrained by the parent more than wholly owned subsidiaries, or is it the other way around?

There is plenty of evidence for the conclusion that formal restraints of this sort are quite common, either by way of licensing agreements or by other formal contracts. But the incidence of such formal restraints can easily be misinterpreted. The purpose of restraints of this sort, of course, is to safeguard the parent against a number of contingencies, including the possibility that the parent may lose control over its international marketing strategy. But the principal contingency that explains such formal restraints is the possibility of subsequent expropriation or forced sale of the subsidiaries. Obviously, a rational parent will sell from any facility that offers the greatest advantages. There is no rationality in excluding any subsidiary from the role if it is an efficient producer; and there is more rationality in assigning profitable opportunity to a wholly owned subsidiary than to a joint venture. But these decisions can be made by the parent even if they are contrary to formal territorial restrictions that were previously placed on the subsidiary. Accordingly, compilations of the existence of geographical restraints are unreliable as indicators of actual company policy. The only general proposition that can be stated with any degree of assurance in this field is that formal restraints imposed upon joint ventures are more likely to signal an actual allocation of markets than formal restraints imposed upon wholly owned subsidiaries.

A special problem that has begun to emerge with respect to joint ventures has proved deeply troubling in a number of less developed countries. Here and there, one discerns the appearance of an indigenous business class whose fortunes are based upon an ability to make themselves acceptable, both to foreigners and government officials, as "safe" local partners. Their object in acquiring the equity of foreign subsidiaries, naturally enough, is to serve their interests as individuals. Whether that interest is in harmony with the interest of the country as a whole is a separate question, with an indeterminate answer.

A final point that bears on the wisdom of a joint-venture policy has to do with the social opportunity cost of the capital involved in the acquisition of the joint ventures. If the equity that falls into local hands is acquired without cost, of course, the advantages to the country of having the equity may be considerable. If, however, the commitment to a joint venture also involves the diversion of local savings from some other local purpose, one has to weigh whether the activity that has been denied the local funds, would serve a better social purpose than the use to which the funds were put. There is no simple answer to that question; but unavoidably there would be some individual cases in which that kind of query would suggest the undesirability of insisting upon a joint venture.

It is only a step from a policy of requiring joint ventures in certain cases to a policy of requiring the actual divestiture of all foreign ownership at some stage in the evolution of an enterprise. There may be a good case for persuading foreigners to relinquish their control over production facilities at some stage in the development of a given line of activity. At the point at which the foreign-owned enterprise no longer has anything further to offer in capital, or technology, or access to markets, the interests of the host government may well be served by persuading the foreigner to move on to other activities where a contribution was more likely. If the transition could be arranged by means that did not discourage other foreigners from setting up needed enterprises in the country, such an outcome might represent the best of all possible worlds from the country's viewpoint.

The fact is that something like this process constantly goes on; but it goes on quite unobtrusively inside the structure of foreign-owned subsidiaries. The product lines of these subsidiaries are not forever frozen. At the stage at which the product becomes fully standardized and begins to lose its oligopolistic characteristics, the interest of the foreign investor in maintaining his position in the local market for the product often declines. In products of that sort, the diseconomies of belonging to a large multinational system may begin to exceed the economies of scale that such a system provides. Accordingly, subsidiaries have been known to slough off products, sometimes voluntarily, sometimes on the urging of host governments. That kind of divestiture is perhaps the safest and simplest from the viewpoint of host governments.

Divestiture of a more obvious sort such as the forced sale of the equity interest in a subsidiary is a more chancy procedure, involving much greater risks for the less developed country. The principal risk, of course, is that the country will be required to divert some of its scarce local saving to the acquisition of foreign-owned properties, and at the same time may be discouraging other foreigners from entering the country. On the other hand, such a step is one that any country is entitled to take, assuming it is prepared to bear the economic costs that might ensue.

The formulation and management of a set of policies with respect to foreign-owned enterprises are burdened with the memories and connotations that surround issues of colonialism and of economic dependence. Policy making in this field is complicated even more by the fact that in local politics foreigners do not vote. Hence, in the byplay of national politics, the parties are sorely tempted to raise issues regarding policies toward foreigners at any stage at which domestic political advantage can be gained. That fact tends to intermingle the genuine and legitimate concerns of thoughtful men over the consequences of foreign investment with the short-term expediencies and gambits of the political process itself. Countries are entitled to decide for themselves how to rate the conflicting values that are always involved in the formulation of policy in this field: the values of growth, of equitable distribution of income, and of tolerable distribution of political influence and social recognition. The views of outsiders over which value should predominate are of no great relevance, especially if those views are based upon self-interest or upon a difference in value systems. Still, even an outsider is entitled to note that policies with respect to foreign investment which prevail in less developed countries are sometimes inimical to the very goals they are intended to serve. In a situation of that sort, men of goodwill can engage in a fruitful exchange of ideas.

The Economic Consequences Of U.S. Foreign Direct Investment

(Reprinted from U.S. Commission for International Trade . . .
Report to The President submitted by the Commission
on International Trade and Investment Policy, 1971)

The Economic Consequences Of U.S. Foreign Direct Investment

This paper summarizes the main economic consequences that seem to be associated with the foreign direct investment of the United States since World War II. It is concerned principally with direct investment in manufacturing. And the economic consequences to which it gives greatest attention are those that appear to have the most immediate bearing on the formulation of U.S. trade policy.[1]

I. The Place of Direct Investment

We begin with the statement of an elementary point, but one of profound importance in the present context.

The act of establishing a foreign subsidiary is something fundamentally different, in both its economic and business implications, from the act of making a portfolio investment overseas. The establishment of a subsidiary generally implies a number of different things: it suggests that an entity is being created on foreign soil which a U.S. enterprise proposes to endow with some physical assets, or with funds to acquire some physical assets; but it suggests also that the

---

[1] This paper draws on materials developed for the book entitled *Sovereignty at Bay: The Multinational Spread of U.S. Enterprises* (New York: Basic Books, 1971) , as part of the product of the multinational enterprise study at the Harvard Business School.

entity will be linked in some sort of common strategy with other units in a multinational system, performing the roles that are assigned to it on behalf of the system as a whole. We shall be elaborating those points later on in this paper. But even without that elaboration, it is evident that in order to evaluate the consequences of encouraging or discouraging the establishment of overseas subsidiaries, one has to address himself to a much wider range of questions than those relating to the international flow of finance capital alone.

There is a second point that needs to be stressed in this context. Any one of the activities associated with foreign direct investment could conceivably be performed by means other than the direct investment route. Producers in foreign countries can obtain funds from the U.S. economy, either directly through loans and grants or indirectly through U.S.-financed international agencies. Foreign producers can secure technological and managerial information by a dozen different routes that do not involve an organic tie with a U.S. parent, including the hiring of individual foreign experts, the purchase of technology in a package deal with foreign equipment, or the negotiation of a licensing agreement with a foreign firm. It is even possible, though a little more difficult, for independent foreign producers to link themselves to a U.S. enterprise in a long-run strategic arrangement, using financing and purchasing contracts as the link.

These alternative channels, to be sure, are more readily available in some industries than in others. As the account below will indicate, the alternatives to multinational enterprises are most readily available in industries that produce a well-standardized product on a relatively competitive basis, and least available for industries that are highly innovative and strongly oligopolistic. As a general rule, however, multinational enterprises are to be found most commonly in the innovative and oligopolistic industries; their importance in the industries with standardized, price-competitive products is very much lower. As a consequence, according to a number of careful studies, multinational enterprises are found principally in industries that devote a relatively high proportion of their resources to research and advertising and that tend to be dominated by very large firms. These are the tendencies that lie behind the distribution by industries of 187 multinational enterprises, found in Table 1.[2]

To a considerable extent, therefore, multinational enterprises are not at the heart of the "trade problem," as generally conceived in the United States. It is true, of course, that there are some enterprises in the group that specialize in problem products: Genesco in shoes, Sylvania in simple electronics, and so on. In general, however, the concentration of these enterprises is in other products. And, on any reasonable assumption about the future, as the analysis below suggests, multinational enterprises are likely to continue to avoid the products which constitute the problem products of U.S. trade policy.

One may query, therefore, whether it makes much sense to think of the multinational enterprise as a useful focus for concern in the context of a review of U.S. trade policy. Much more to the point, it may be, are questions such as the following: should U.S. interests be allowed to export finance capital to industrial borrowers abroad, whatever the route; should they be allowed to export management and technological skills, whatever the means; should they be allowed to enter into organic strategic ties with foreign producers, whatever the form?

Obviously, this paper is not intended to pursue questions of such breadth. In confining itself to the multinational enterprise, however, there is a risk that it may be nibbling at the edge of the issue as perceived in the United States.

---

[2] The 187 U.S. enterprises in that table represent all the enterprises in *Fortune's 500* industrials of 1963 or 1964 that at any time had manufacturing subsidiaries in six or more countries.

TABLE 1

187 U.S.-Controlled Multinational Enterprises
Compared with All U.S. Enterprises, by Industry, 1966
(*Dollars in Billions*)

Industry (SIC)	187 Enterprises			All U.S. Enterprises		187 Enterprises as Percent of All Enterprises	
	Number of Enterprises	Sales	Assets	Sales	Assets	Sales	Assets
Motor vehicles & equipment (371)	11	$41.9	$26.9	$49.6	$31.2	84.5	86.2
Drugs (283)	15	5.5	4.3	7.2	5.8	76.5	74.2
Fabricated metal products (34)	10	5.0	3.7	6.6	4.4	75.9	84.1
Petroleum refining (29)	9	31.7	42.1	46.4	61.4	68.5	68.6
Chemicals (minus drugs) (other 28)	25	22.3	21.6	37.3	33.5	59.5	64.5
Rubber and miscellaneous plastic products (30)	5	7.7	5.9	13.5	9.1	57.1	64.8
Electrical mach., equip. & supplies (36)	19	24.5	20.9	49.2	32.7	49.8	64.0
Instruments & related products (38)	5	4.5	3.9	11.2	8.6	40.2	45.4
Nonelectrical machinery (35)	20	15.4	13.2	48.2	33.9	32.1	38.9
Food & kindred products (20)	29	24.5	12.1	77.6	34.0	31.5	35.6
Primary nonferrous metals (333)	7	4.6	5.4	15.8	14.5	28.1	24.8
Aircraft & parts (372)	4	5.4	2.3	19.2	12.6	28.1	18.3
Stone, clay, & glass (32)	7	3.7	3.4	14.1	12.7	26.2	26.8
Paper & allied products (26)	5	3.7	3.5	17.0	14.6	21.8	24.0

Other transportation equipment (other 37)	3	1.0	1.1	5.8	4.8	17.2	22.9
Leather products (31)	1	0.8	0.3	5.9	2.7	13.5	11.1
Misc. mfg. & ordnance (39)	2	0.8	0.9	8.1	5.4	9.8	16.7
Lumber–wood prod., excl. furn. (24)	1	0.8	1.0	9.1	6.5	8.8	15.4
Furniture & fixtures (25)	2	0.6	0.4	6.8	3.2	8.8	12.5
Tobacco manufacturing (21)	1	0.5	0.5	6.5	4.5	7.7	11.1
Textile mill & apparel products (22 & 23)	4	2.2	1.8	37.6	18.8	5.9	9.6
Primary iron & steel (331)	1	1.2	1.3	26.2	23.6	4.6	5.2
Printing & publishing, excl. news. (27)	1	0.5	0.4	13.1	8.3	3.8	4.8
Total	187	208.8	176.9	532.0	386.8	39.2	45.7

SOURCE: For 187 enterprise data, *Fortune*, Vol. LXXV, No. 7, 1967, p. 196 *et seq*.; for all U.S. enterprise data, *FTC-SEC Quarterly Financial Report on Manufacturing*, 4th quarter, 1966.

II. The Basic Multinationalizing Forces

To understand the relationship of U.S. foreign direct investment to the U.S. economy, it helps to identify the forces behind the multinationalizing movement.

The Historical Patterns

Multinational activities on the part of U.S. enterprises are, of course, nothing very new. Even before World War II, U.S. enterprises had set up a considerable number of manufacturing subsidiaries in overseas markets. By 1939, for instance, the 187 leading U.S. manufacturers covered in Table 1 already had established 715 manufacturing subsidiaries outside the United States: 335 in Europe; 169 in Canada; 114 in Latin America; and the rest in other parts of the globe. At that time, U.S. parents in the aggregate carried their foreign direct investments on their books at a value just under $4 billion; but the likelihood is that even in 1939 their actual stake in these enterprises was already considerably larger.

This commitment to overseas manufacturing had accumulated over a very long period of time. Beginning in the 1870s, companies like Colt Arms, Singer Sewing Machine, Westinghouse, International Paper, and many others had sensed the opportunity and need to set up overseas production facilities, as a means of prolonging their hold on existing export markets or of penetrating new ones.[3] Like their

[3] The story of the period prior to World War II can be pieced together from many sources including: Mira Wilkins, *The Emergence of Multinational Enterprise* (Cambridge: Harvard University Press, 1970) ; Mira Wilkins and F. E. Hill, *American Business Abroad: Ford on Six Continents* (Detroit: Wayne State University Press, 1964) ; Nathan Rosenberg, "The Role of Technology in American Economic Growth," in *A New American Economic History* (New York: Harper & Row, 1971) ; ——— "Technological Change in the Machine Tool Industry, 1840–1910," in the *Journal of Economic History*, Vol. XXIII, No. 4, December 1963, p. 414; ———, (with Edward Ames) , "The Enfield Arsenal in Theory and History," *Economic Journal*, Vol. LXXVIII,

followers nearly a century later, the U.S. parent involved in these early investments had managed to acquire some organizational or technological capability as a result of earlier successes in the United States market. In some instances, the "advantage" was based on the mastery of a technical process that few others had achieved; in some instances, on the achievement of an organizational capability, such as a unique capability for collecting and using information or a capability for maintaining an efficient network of distributors; and in some instances, on the development of a trade name on which buyers had some substantial confidence. These U.S. parents, therefore, characteristically came out of industries that were highly concentrated in their industrial structure and that were dominated by relatively large firms.

Before setting up their subsidiaries abroad, many of these enterprises had already penetrated foreign markets by way of exports. The immediate action that led such firms to shift from an export position to local production was usually their perception of the threat arising from local competition. Sometimes this threat of competition was made all the more real by the decision of foreign countries to raise their import restrictions of U.S. exports; but sometimes not.

In other cases, however, the stimulating force was at least as much a perception of opportunity as it was a response to threat. Firms that saw themselves beginning to exhaust their

---

December 1968, p. 837 and ———, "Introduction" in the *American System of Manufactures* (Edinburgh: Edinburgh University Press, 1969). Other well-known sources have also helped greatly, including especially J. H. Habbakuk, *American and British Technology in the Nineteenth Century* (Cambridge, England: University Press, 1962); W. P. Strassmann, *Risk and Technological Innovation* (Ithaca: Cornell University Press, 1959); A. L. Levine, *Industrial Retardation in Britain 1880–1914* (New York: Basic Books, 1967); D. H. Aldcroft (ed.), *The Development of British Industry and Foreign Competition 1875–1914* (Toronto: University of Toronto Press, 1968); Frank Southard, *American Industry in Europe* (Boston: Houghton Mifflin, 1931); D. M. Phelps, *Migration of Industry to Latin America* (New York: McGraw-Hill, 1936).

prospects for exploiting the special technology or special ability of the enterprise in the U.S. market looked to new markets in which to profit from these intangible assets.

Why did U.S. enterprises take such an early and commanding lead in overseas direct investment, in a period when the U.S. economy as a whole was still a "debtor country"? The answer is worth stressing because the basic reason seems to have persisted up to the present day. The reason seems to lie in the nature of the skills that U.S. firms had developed as a result of their intimate contact with the U.S. market. Those skills were distinctly different in certain critical respects from the skills that European firms were simultaneously developing. And the difference was due to the fact that American business before World War II confronted a national economy that was different in some respects from that of Europe.

Remember that the industrial tradition of Britain, Germany, and France goes back much earlier than that of the United States. When the era of the modern factory arrived in the 19th century, those countries already possessed a rich supply of artisan skills that carried over from their earlier process of industrialization. The Americans on the other hand were short of all kinds of labor, especially labor that was trained to some professional artisan task. At the same time, the Americans had both a per capita income and a level of general literacy that was the match of the Europeans; indeed, from at least 1870 on, U.S. per capita income was perceptibly higher than that of the Europeans. U.S. businessmen, therefore, were faced with an opportunity to sell to a large and expanding market, comprised of consumers whose tastes were being shaped by the highest per capita income in the world. At the same time, they were handicapped in the satisfaction of those needs by the fact that they did not have Europe's rich supply of relatively skilled and relatively inexpensive labor on which to draw.

Long before World War II, the response of U.S. manufacturers for dealing with their labor scarcities was one that still can be seen under current conditions. The answer was to subdivide the complex skills of manufacturing into many smaller tasks; to standardize each small task into a routine operation; and to use semi-skilled production workers to perform those tasks on a repetitive, routine basis. This meant the development of production processes, machine characteristics, and final product characteristics that were rather different from those which prevailed in Europe. The machines we created to meet our needs were a great deal more highly specialized than the Europeans'; and the labor demanded in the operation of the machines was measurably less skilled. If there were any drawbacks in this choice, they lay in the fact that machines of this type are generally relatively wasteful of raw materials as compared with machines operated by workers with a more artisan bent. And, as a rule, they generally involved more capital per unit of output. But raw materials, if not capital, were generally in plentiful supply in the United States.

The innovational stimuli that were operating on U.S. businessmen, it should be noted, were producing products with a relatively assured future. Products wanted by a market with the highest per capita income in the world were products that others were likely eventually to want, once their income was high enough. And innovations that offered the promise of saving on labor had an especially promising future. The price of labor had been going up relative to the price of capital and materials from 1850 onward, both in Europe and in North America. Accordingly, the conditions of the U.S. market have fortuitously given American businessmen the kind of stimulus to innovations that in general have had a promising future in international markets.

To be sure, Europeans have been far from idle in the field of industrial innovation. Before World War II, they had already made their mark with advances in the field of drugs, synthetic dyestuffs, fertilizer, plastics, and steel. Indeed, there was almost no field of invention, including fields that were labor-conserving in character, in which they had not made some contribution. But many labor-saving inventions were abandoned by Europeans before they could be brought to a marketable state; and many others were taken up for large-scale exploitation first by U.S. businessmen for the U.S. market, even though invented by Europeans. Those that have forged ahead in Europe, it should be noted, were commonly material-saving in character.

The result has been that American enterprises in years gone by have had a much larger menu of innovations on the basis of which they might penetrate the European market than was the case for the Europeans. While the United States was able to develop a European market for its manufactured products principally on the basis of the novel aspects of its products, the Europeans acquired their markets in the United States principally on the basis of lower costs of manufacture.

One way of generalizing the resulting patterns of trade before World War II is presented in Figure 1.

As the figure shows, U.S. production tended to exceed its consumption in the early stages following the introduction of a new product. The characteristic pattern for the United States at that stage was to build up exports to other countries, mainly to Canada and Western Europe. However, at some point, U.S. enterprises began to sense the need for local production: partly in response to the appearance of local imitators, partly out of a fear that imitation would soon begin. Thereafter, exports tended to diminish; indeed, in a few cases, such as in various lines of office machinery, the net export pattern turned to net imports. Even when the United States did not become a net importer, however, U.S. enterprises began to use their European subsidiaries for the pro-

FIGURE 1. Patterns of Trade Before World War II

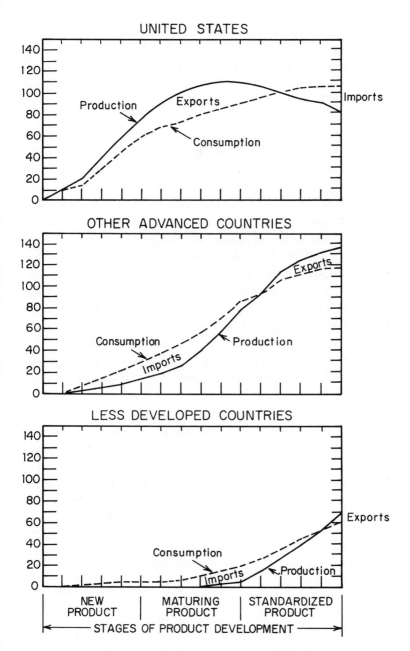

UNITED STATES

OTHER ADVANCED COUNTRIES

LESS DEVELOPED COUNTRIES

visioning of third-country markets, such as the markets of the Commonwealth, Asia, and Africa.

Whereas the pattern before World War II is derived from unsystematic and anecdotal materials, that after the war is better documented. In substance, the basic pattern seems to have carried over into the postwar period, along with new developments that were a logical and consistent extension of the old.

One study indicative of the continuation of the old trends deals with a group of consumer durable products that were first introduced in commercial markets 20 or 25 years ago.[4] According to this study, the change in U.S. export patterns between the early 1950s and the early 1960s could be predicted mainly on the basis of two characteristics of the products: whether these products in the first instance represented items associated with high-income consumers; and how long the products had been on the market. The more these products were identified with high-income users and the briefer their period of existence, the stronger was the U.S. export position. Changes in the U.S. export position between the early 1950s and the early 1960s could be explained principally on the basis of the maturation of the product in world markets, without reference to any data on relative production cost levels.

Another study, dealing with nine major petrochemicals, produced similar results.[5] This study demonstrated a number of different things that are central to the issue here: first, the fact that the United States was a large net exporter of these petrochemicals only as long as there were few outside imitators of the production technology; second, that once the imitators appeared, U S. firms responded defensively by

---

[4] L. T. Wells, Jr., "Product Innovation and Directions of International Trade" (unpublished D.B.A. thesis, Harvard Business School, 1966).

[5] R. B. Stobaugh, "The Product Life Cycle, U.S. Exports, and International Investment" (unpublished D.B.A. thesis, Harvard Business School, 1968).

setting up a considerable number of subsidiaries abroad; third, that this was followed by a new pattern of international trade, in which U.S. exports reappeared from time to time, mainly when there were temporary surpluses in productive capacity in the United States; and, finally, that the imitators managed in the end to appropriate the technology and to obtain a share of the markets that U.S.-owned plants had previously reserved to themselves.

Numerous other studies support the general plausibility of the underlying assumption that the U.S. trade position in manufactured goods is based heavily on a comparative advantage in the generation of innovations, rather than on the more conventional notion of relatively cheap capital. These studies indicate that U.S. exports of manufactured goods depend critically upon product differentiation; that this relative emphasis is less marked for other advanced countries than for the United States, which appears to rely much more on price differences as a basis for its exports; and that once the product has begun to age, imitators commonly preempt the market which U.S. exports may have built up in foreign economies. Some of the studies that support elements of this complex hypothesis are analyses of individual industries; [6] some are more general in character.[7]

----

[6] In addition to those cited earlier, see G. C. Hufbauer, *Synthetic Materials and the Theory of International Trade* (London: Gerald Duckworth & Co., 1966) ; OECD, *Gaps in Technology Between Member Countries: Sector Report, Plastics* (Paris, 1968) ; Christopher Freeman, studies on the plastics industry, the electronics industry, and the chemical process plant industry, respectively, in the following issues of the *National Institute of Economic Review:* No. 26, November 1963; No. 34, November 1965; and No. 45, August 1968.

[7] H. S. Houthakker and S. P. Magee, "Income and Price Elasticities in World Trade," *The Review of Economics and Statistics*, Vol. LI, No. 2, May 1969, pp. 111–25; F. M. Adler, "The Relationship between the Income and Price Elasticities of Demand for U.S. Exports," November 1969, Columbia University (mimeo.) ; W. H. Branson, *A Disaggregated Model of the U.S. Balance of Trade* (Washington: Federal Reserve System Staff Economic Study, 1968) ; G. C. Hufbauer, "The Impact of National Characteristics and Tech-

This process seems to explain why the big postwar increase in U.S. overseas investment in manufacturing subsidiaries has come about mainly in the kind of industry that would be expected to have participated in such a process: industries associated with innovation and with oligopoly. It explains why so much of the investment is found in the chemical industries, the machinery industries, the transportation industries, and the scientific instrument industries.[8]

Data produced at the Harvard Business School confirm this pattern of specialization from another point of view. They show that of the various product lines introduced for manufacture abroad by U.S. parent firms, more than two-thirds were in "skill-oriented" industries of the sort just listed.[9] Apart from those groups, one found considerable investment mainly in the food products industries, that is, in lines where problems of bulk and weight would have prevented the use of exports as the principal way of exploiting special U.S. skills in production and distribution.

Since this paper is devoted mainly to the trade aspects of foreign direct investment, it may be helpful to recall that the continuous challenge of foreign producers to the innovat-

---

nology on the Commodity Composition of Trade in Manufactured Goods," in Raymond Vernon (ed.), *The Technology Factor in International Trade* (New York: Columbia University Press, 1970) ; in the same volume, W. H. Gruber and Raymond Vernon, "The Technology Factor in a World Trade Matrix"; J. H. Dunning, "European and U.S. Trade Patterns, U.S. Foreign Investment, and the Technological Gap," *Proceedings of the International Economic Association*, September 1969; Yoshihiro Tsurumi, "Technology Transfer and Foreign Trade: The Case of Japan, 1950–1966" (unpublished D.B.A. thesis, Harvard Business School, 1968) .

[8] See also W. H. Gruber, Dileep Mehta, and Raymond Vernon, "The R&D Factor in International Trade and International Investment," *The Journal of Political Economy*, Vol. 75, No. 1, February 1967, pp. 20–37; J. H. Dunning, "Technology, United States Investment and European Economic Growth," in C. P. Kindleberger (ed.), *The International Corporation* (Cambridge: M.I.T. Press, 1970) , pp. 141–76.

[9] There are many definitional and measurement problems that lie behind this concept, but they do not affect the validity of the general statement.

ing "skill-oriented" U.S. industries is not the only challenge that U.S. industries have faced. Obviously, there have also been challenges to the older labor-intensive industries — challenges of a more insistent sort. In these industries, U.S. producers could not fall back on an innovational lead to help them survive. A U.S. firm could not seriously hope that, by setting up an overseas subsidiary, it would outdo rival foreign producers on the basis of some special firm-specific knowledge or firm-specific skills. In these industries, therefore, a common strategy of U.S. firms has been to enter into purchase arrangements with foreign producers; and if there were some marginal skills that the U.S. firm was in a position to impart, to pass these on by way of informal person-to-person instruction or by way of licensing agreements.

This description of the general relation between U.S. overseas investment and U.S. trade suggests the importance of looking more closely at two factors likely to play a key role in any projection of future trends: first, the "innovation" process, because it seems to figure so centrally in U.S. trade relations with the advanced countries; second, developments among the less developed countries, because these constitute so large a part of the "low-wage" trade issue.

III. Technology and Innovation

Technology and innovation, according to the argument, play a major role in explaining the changing position of the United States in international trade. If that is so, are these factors to be construed as favorable or unfavorable in their effect on the future U.S. trade position? According to some accounts, particularly those emanating from Canada and Europe, the U.S. technological lead threatens to establish a

U.S. economic hegemony over the economies of other countries. According to other accounts, especially those from the United States, a shrinking of the U.S. technological lead promises to undermine the U.S. position in world trade.

To some extent, the product cycle concept, described a few pages earlier, resolves the dispute. It attributes the early lead of U.S. exporters in new products to a technological advantage; and it notes the near-inevitability of the erosion of that lead as its technological base is eaten away through diffusion and imitation. Then, according to the product cycle synthesis, the U.S. producers move on to the generation and export of new products. In this process, the multinational enterprise functions as a critical actor: developing the technology; initially exporting the product; and subsequently producing the product directly in the foreign markets to which it had previously exported.

Note the importance of exports in the pattern so far described. That importance is confirmed by the fact that the multinational enterprises or their overseas affiliates have been involved as parties in about one-half of aggregate U.S. exports in manufactured products, concentrated principally in the more advanced product lines.[10]

Will this relationship continue? To probe that question, one has to consider first of all certain changes in the technological background.

The technological position of the United States has been undergoing rapid change. For one thing, in the period since World War II, the United States has forged ahead in the fields of pure science. From 1951 to 1969, for instance, the United States took 21 of the 38 Nobel Prizes in physics, 9 of the 27 in chemistry, and 23 of the 40 in medicine and

---

[10] Marie T. Bradshaw, "U.S. Exports to Foreign Affiliates of U.S. Firms," *Survey of Current Business*, Vol. 49, No. 5, Part I, May 1969. The same kind of association is noted by various tests conducted as part of the multinational enterprise study by the Harvard Business School.

physiology. This is a new role for the U.S. in the history of science.

History tells us, however, that scientific achievements are far from being the same thing as industrial development advances. The fruits of scientific analysis, as a rule, are widely distributed; they are, indeed, a free good to any country that has the capacity for interpreting and absorbing them. In fact, for a long time, the United States left it to the rest of the world to make the bulk of the pure scientific advances, while it partook of some of the fruits at bargain prices; and Japan, in general, is still following that policy.

More to the point, therefore, is the fact that U.S. gross expenditure on "research and development" (most of it being "development") has expanded faster than that of Europe and has come to approximate 15 times that of Germany, 10 times that of the U.K. and 3 times that of all Western Europe combined. Even after adjusting for differences in the purchasing power of the research dollar, the disparity between European and U.S. activity is very large. In addition, the average money commitment involved in the achievement of any major industrial innovation has been growing fairly rapidly. In the nineteenth century, the notion that a Whitney or a Morse or an Edison might develop an idea, carry it through its period of industrial development, and launch it successfully on the market, was not to be excluded; today that possibility has become increasingly unlikely. Small firms with large ideas commonly find it necessary to sell out to the giants, in order to realize the full potential of their innovations.

The reasons for this need are complex and are explored more fully elsewhere.[11] The consequence is that the cost of launching new major products has become very large. A

---

[11] See my article "Organization as a Scale Factor in the Growth of Firms," in J. W. Markham and G. F. Papanek (eds.), *Industrial Organization and Economic Development* (Boston: Houghton Mifflin Company, 1970).

typical illustration is DuPont's post-invention cost in the development of orlon, reported at about $5 million in dollars of 1940 vintage.[12] IBM is said to have spent $2 to $5 billion in developing the third generation computer (though it is not altogether clear just what the figure covers). And the development of the Concorde air frame, according to some seemingly careful estimates, cost in the neighborhood of $2 billion.[13]

The case of the Concorde illustrates the fact that it is not only money but also organizational time and organizational commitment that are involved. That plane will have taken at least a decade for development before it is available for commercial use. Other major inventions, such as the video taperecorder, oral contraceptives, and the electron microscope, all post-World War II inventions, yield estimates of the same order of magnitude.[14] While it could not be said that the large U.S. enterprises are more efficient in the generation of new ideas or in the spending of research funds, it seems fairly clear that their scale has given them an advantage in the subsequent process of developing and marketing their new products.

Since leading U.S. enterprises are characteristically about twice as large as those in the same industries in Europe,[15] the

---

[12] W. F. Mueller, "The Origins of the Basic Inventions Underlying DuPont's Major Product and Process Innovations, 1920 to 1950," in R. R. Nelson (ed.), *The Rate and Direction of Inventive Activity* (Princeton: Princeton University Press, 1962), p. 337.

[13] "Concorde's Growing Pay Load," *The Economist*, August 16–22, 1969, p. 51.

[14] Edwin Mansfield, *The Economics of Technological Change* (New York: W. W. Norton & Co., 1968), pp. 84–86; Illinois Institute of Technology Research (IIT), *TRACES: Technology in Retrospect and Critical Events in Science* (Chicago: December 1968), prepared under NSF contract C535, pp. iv–ix, 12, 17.

[15] S. H. Hymer and Robert Rowthorn, *Multinational Corporations and International Oligopoly: The Non-American Challenge*, Center Discussion Paper No. 75, September 1969, Economic Growth Center, Yale University, 1969, Tables 5 and 6.

increasing need for scale does seem to have added to the U.S. position of strength. Nor is there much evidence that the Europeans will rapidly close the size gap between themselves and the leading U.S. firms. Although mergers are occurring in Europe, they are occurring with difficulty. Moreover, there are still very few cases in which the developmental and innovational work of "merged" European firms has been genuinely integrated. At the same time, governmental and intergovernmental institutions in Europe seem unable to generate research programs in the public sector that are comparable in size and creative drive with those being supported by the U.S. government.

Nevertheless, the trends bearing on projections for the future do not all run one way. There is some evidence that new products and processes, once introduced, tend to be adopted faster than was once the case — roughly twice as rapidly after World War II as in the interwar period.[16] More rapid adoption almost certainly means more rapid diffusion of the industrial innovation. And rapid diffusion, in turn, probably means that the period is somewhat shortened in which an innovator can hope to exploit his lead in comparative peace. Once multiple sources of a technology are in existence, the chance that a multinational enterprise can dominate the market on a basis of its technological lead rapidly fades. U.S. enterprises, therefore, may be able to count on generating many new innovational leads; but they will also have to anticipate that the challenges of their marketing positions in products they had introduced will come earlier in the life of the product. In the end, some of the challenged lines will be curtailed or abandoned, as the enterprise turns its organizational energies to more promising lines.

---

[16] Frank Lynn, "The Rate of Development and Diffusion of Technology," in H. R. Bowen and G. L. Mangum, *Automation and Economic Progress* (Englewood Cliffs, N.J.: Prentice-Hall, 1966) , pp. 99–113.

The cases that are at the center of present U.S. trade problems, as a rule, come from two sources. Either they come from the older lines of manufactured products in which U.S. enterprises are losing a once-held technical advantage (such as vitamins and transistors), or they are the products of industries that are not identified with a strong innovative drive (such as clothing and steel). A strong U.S. innovational lead in steel was last seen in the early 1920s, with the introduction of the continuous hot strip mill, and it is not clear that such a lead will soon reappear. A U.S. lead in clothing could well be based on advances in the field of synthetic fibers, but it can hardly be expected to be large or vigorous. In lines such as these, independent producers outside the United States can secure their technology from numerous sources in the United States, Western Europe, and Japan. In many cases, it is not even a question of securing technology as a separate product; the needed technology is built into the capital equipment, and the equipment is widely available on a highly competitive basis. Where the equipment needs to be supplemented by some kind of training from other countries, there is no difficulty in arranging for that training.[17]

In industries that produce a well-standardized product, therefore, countries outside the United States stand a good chance of producing as cheaply as the United States. Indeed, if there is any significant amount of labor needed in the production process, they stand a good chance of producing at costs lower than those in the United States. To block that possibility, controls over multinational enterprises would be almost irrelevant. What would be needed would be a return to the world of the Luddites, with strict controls over the international movement of knowledge in any form, whether through the multinational enterprise or otherwise.

---

[17] J. L. Espy, "The Strategies of Chinese Industrial Enterprises in Hong Kong," (unpublished D.B.A. thesis, Harvard Business School, 1970).

IV. The Less Developed Areas

Another subject for close attention, as noted earlier, is the change in the position of some of the less developed areas since World War II, especially in relation to U.S. trade and manufacturing investment. In this case, the concern runs along different lines. Even without any change in technology, these countries could constitute a rising threat for U.S. industry. All one needs to assume in order to generate such worries is: (a) that U.S. industry is developing a greater capacity for scanning the world in order to exploit the opportunities offered by the less developed areas; or (b) that the areas are increasing their technical capabilities to serve such needs, without commensurately increasing their costs. In this instance, too, some historical background will place the issues in better perspective.

Even before World War II, U.S. enterprises had undertaken some investment in manufacturing facilities in less developed areas. Some of these cases represented investments that were incidental to the acquisition and processing of raw materials: sugar processing mills, copper smelting facilities, and the like. Others represented a response to the heavy costs of transportation associated with certain exports from the United States: electric elevators, automobiles, and a few other bulky products of that sort. A very few represented the defensive responses of U.S. firms to new import restrictions in the less developed areas; these characteristically, were "modern" products, but products that had reached a reasonably standardized stage, such as paints and consumer durables.

All told, however, the investments were not very significant. The Department of Commerce data, which probably understate the figures somewhat, report a total investment by U.S. parents in the less developed areas, on the order of

$350 million as of 1940. The Harvard study of the operations of 187 large U.S. parents indicates that by 1939 about 150 manufacturing subsidiaries had been created or acquired in those areas. Since a few of these subsidiaries produced more than one product line, the number of country product lines came to 185 for the group.

Contrary to general impression, there was a great burst of activity on the part of U.S. parents, during the twenty-odd years following the end of World War II, in the establishment of manufacturing subsidiaries in less developed areas. By 1967, the total investment figure had gone up to $6.3 billion; the number of subsidiaries of the 187 large firms covered by the Harvard study had increased to 300; and the number of product lines had increased even more substantially to over 900.

Several forces contributed to this sharp expansion. In the first place, the U.S. parents involved in these operations were changing internally in such way that the function of scanning overseas markets for threats and opportunities was now being done much more systematically and at higher level in the enterprise; that capability inside the firm was being accelerated by declines in the money cost and time cost of transportation and communication. In addition, however, the governments of the less developed countries were engaging in a series of new policies that rapidly increased both the threats and the opportunities as seen through the eyes of the U.S. parents.

The developments inside the U.S. parent firms that had elevated the overseas scanning process to a high-level activity have been well-documented in other studies.[18] The fact that

---

[18] J. M. Stopford, "Growth and Organizational Change in the Multinational Firm" (unpublished D.B.A. thesis, Harvard Business School, 1968) ; Lawrence Franko, "Strategy Choice and Multinational Corporate Tolerance for Joint Ventures with Foreign Partners" (unpublished D.B.A. thesis, Harvard Business School, 1970) .

costs of transportation and communication were declining in relation to other costs is a phenomenon that need not be documented extensively here; and the fact that this force is likely to continue, perhaps at an accelerated rate, seems a plausible assumption for the future. However, the second factor — the systematic use of policies by less developed countries aimed at speeding up industrialization — merits a word or two of elaboration.

Since World War II, the larger and least backward of the less developed countries have been developing a considerable capacity for manufacturing. Nations like Mexico, Brazil, Argentina, Tunisia, Nigeria, Turkey, and India have produced an industrial class and a related infrastructure that are capable of absorbing technology and managing plants, especially in products that present no overwhelming technological or organizational difficulties. As these capabilities have grown among the less developed countries, their governments have tended to adopt policies that would encourage local production and reduce imports of manufactured goods. A period of protection, it was assumed, would be required in order to offset the initial lead of the foreigners based upon scale economies and to offset the consumer preference for long-established foreign trade names. Most governments at first were indifferent to the question whether local production would eventually be able to generate costs and prices that were competitive with foreign products; but some displayed a certain sensitivity to this question. In any event, a very widespread policy among the upper range of less-developed countries has been the institution of regimes of heavy import protection. And the response of U.S. parents to such policies has been to set up subsidiaries inside those markets.

Almost invariably, the cost structures of these subsidiaries during the early years of their existence have been very high. Those elevated costs have been a result of a number of different factors: the high level of duties that were imposed on imported intermediate products; the small scale of internal markets; and the general overvaluation of the currencies of many of the countries concerned.[19]

As a general rule, when U.S. parents first introduced their manufacturing subsidiaries in less developed areas, their intention was that these subsidiaries should confine their activities principally to the provisioning of local markets. The usual experience, however, has been one in which costs have tended to decline over time, as the subsidiaries have gained more experience in the local economies and as the level of their production has gone up.[20] As a result, a number of U.S. parents have found themselves considering the possibility that subsidiaries in less developed countries might be able to perform efficiently the function that their European subsidiaries had earlier taken up, namely, the function of producing for export markets. Serious consideration of that possibility has been accelerated in some countries, such as Mexico and India, which have insisted upon such exports as a condition of access to local markets.

In some countries, of course, it took no special urging on the part of the host governments to stimulate U.S. parents to produce for export. In Taiwan, Korea, Hong Kong, and Singapore, for instance, the attractiveness of using well-disciplined, hard-working unskilled labor to perform standardized tasks was self-evident. Here and there, too, some special

---

[19] For illustrative materials, see Jack Baranson, *Automotive Industries in Developing Countries* (Baltimore: Johns Hopkins Press, 1969); Ayhan Cilingiroglu, *Manufacture of Heavy Electrical Equipment in Developing Countries* (Baltimore: Johns Hopkins Press, 1969); Jack Baranson, *Manufacturing Problems in India* (Syracuse: Syracuse University Press, 1967); G. S. Edelberg, "The Procurement Practices of the Mexican Affiliates of Selected United States Automobile Firms" (unpublished D.B.A. thesis, Harvard Business School, 1963).

[20] Unfortunately, there is no systematic data on this very critical point. For suggestive indications, however, see the Baranson and Cilingiroglu studies cited earlier.

governmental exemptions or other advantages were added to the attractiveness of the availability of low-cost labor; the free trade zones of Mexico's northern border, for instance, was one such attractive situation. All these forces combined to push U.S. parents into a new phase in their global planning.

The effect of employing the less developed areas for the export of manufactured products has begun to be apparent in the trade data reported from various countries. A comprehensive study covering Latin America, conducted by the U.S. Department of Commerce for 1966, indicates that about 41 percent of the exports of manufactured products from Latin American countries in that year were accounted for by the local subsidiaries of U.S. enterprises, even though the proportion of total manufacturers of those enterprises in the area amounted to only 10 percent.[21]

A comprehensive global survey of manufactured goods exported from the less developed countries suggests more of the same pattern. Apart from the Latin Americans, according to this survey, India and Southeast Asia have contributed heavily to the growth in export of manufactured goods. The products involved have been in the standardized well-established categories, but they have included items of increasing sophistication, such as office machines, telecommunications equipment, and motorcycles. Increasingly, the destinations of the products have been the markets of advanced countries; and throughout the process, the subsidiaries of foreign-owned enterprises have played a leading role.[22]

---

[21] Council for Latin America, *The Effects of United States and Other Foreign Investment in Latin America,* January 1970. The Latin American data are especially impressive because they indicate that between 1957 and 1966, about 65 percent of the $900 million increase in Latin American exports of manufactures was to be attributed to the local subsidiaries of the U.S. parent companies.

[22] GATT Secretariat, "Engineering Export Patterns," *International Trade Forum,* Vol. VI, No. 1, February 1970, pp. 17–26. A recent survey of India's

There is not much doubt about the generalization to be drawn from these data. The less developed world is now well within the planning horizons of U.S. parents and within the logistical systems they have developed. But an important inference should not be overlooked. U.S. markets are well within the scanning capabilities of other producers in these areas, whether or not they are associated with multinational enterprises, or they soon will become so. The problem, if it is a problem, is one that is generated by an increasingly open world, a trend of which the multinational enterprise is only one manifestation.

V. An Economic Appraisal

Despite the fact that the multinational enterprise phenomenon has to be viewed as a manifestation of a much more general process, it may be helpful to review what economists think its economic effects have been. This is a difficult and murky field, but there are a few solid points that can be extracted from the work done so far.

Nature of the Transaction

In order to make some kind of systematic evaluation of the effects of the creation of multinational enterprises on the U.S. economy, one has to begin by recalling the basic point with which this paper began. Economists had long been disposed to look upon the creation of foreign subsidiaries very much as they would upon a portfolio investment: as nothing more than a sum of money transferred from the United States

---

engineering goods industries underlines the key role of foreign-owned subsidiaries in their growing exports. R. K. Singh, "Engineering Goods Export and Foreign Collaboration," *Calcutta Statesman,* 1970, date and page undetermined.

for investment in another country. Businessmen will recognize at once that this way of looking on this creation of an overseas subsidiary has little to do with reality. While subsidiaries may be endowed with some sum of money at the outset, the important endowments are of other kinds: access to the parents' store of technical skills, to the parents' organizational apparatus for search, and to the markets provided by the parents' downstream subsidiaries. If large sums of money are required for the conduct of the subsidiary's affairs, the characteristic disposition of parents is to try to raise the funds in the local market, if it can be done. As a result, for every dollar that moves from the United States to foreign countries in connection with the financing of overseas manufacturing subsidiaries, something like three or four dollars are raised for these subsidiaries outside the United States.[23] Needless to say, the same thing is true of manpower: the 49,000 Americans employed in U.S.-controlled foreign subsidiaries in 1966 appear to have been associated with the employment of some 5.5 million local workers.[24] Therefore, the real value of the subsidiary, whether to the U.S. economy or to the host country, can hardly be measured by reference to the size of the capital sum that happened to cross the U.S. borders at the time of its establishment; the real value has to be measured by determining the marginal consequences of setting up the subsidiary, attaching it to the multinational enterprise, and

---

[23] These estimates are based on the "sources and uses of funds" analysis for 1958–1965, published in various issues of the *Survey of Current Business* and presented in summary in G. C. Hufbauer and F. M. Adler, *Overseas Manufacturing Investment and the Balance of Payments* (Washington: U.S. Treasury Department, 1968) , p. 16.

[24] These estimates are built up from: "American Overseas," Selected Area Report PC (3) –1C, U.S. *Census of Population* (Washington: GPO, 1964) , Table 16; Department of Commerce, *U.S. Bureau Investment in Foreign Countries* (Washington: GPO, 1960) ; Council for Latin America, *The Effects of United States and Other Foreign Investment in Latin America* (New York, 1970) , pp. 84–89.

putting its complex mixture of foreign and local resources to work as part of the global structure.

Measuring the Consequences

How to measure those complex consequences is baffling. A subsidiary, it is important to note, is not necessarily a meaningful unit in strategic business terms. Some subsidiaries earn their way in a multinational system simply because they are responsible for a learning process from which the system as a whole hopes eventually to profit; a Mexican subsidiary, for instance, may be used as a staging area for eventual expansion into other countries of Latin America. An automobile assembly plant or a pharmaceutical processing plant may be justified primarily by the profits it generates in the manufacture of components in other countries. Accordingly, there is no a priori reason to equate the earnings of a subsidiary with the advantages that the multinational enterprise as a whole derives from the subsidiary. Nor is there any basis for assuming any simple consequences based on the concept of a zero-sum game, such as the notion that what is produced by such a subsidiary abroad would otherwise have been produced by the parent in the United States. Indeed, there are no economic models as yet sufficiently subtle and dynamic to capture the medium-term and long-term consequences of creating an overseas subsidiary. In the end, the decision whether to support or retard this kind of development on the part of U.S. enterprises must be made by what amounts to an intuitive leap.

Observe another aspect of the measurement problem. In order to measure the effects on the U.S. economy of the development of its multinational enterprises, one has to answer the question: "As compared with what?" If multinational enterprises had not developed, U.S. business would turn its resources and its energies in other directions. But what would these directions be? Would U.S. management place much more emphasis on cost-cutting innovations in the United States, in an effort to become competitive on a price basis? Would it engage far more extensively in licensing its industrial innovations? Or would the individuals involved offer their personal services to foreign economies on a very much larger scale, as some chemical and engineering firms have been known to do? Unless the alternatives are explicitly specified, one cannot claim to be measuring the effects of the development of multinational enterprises upon the U.S. economy.

Still, there are a few slight indications of the direction of those effects. Perhaps the most systematic effect in this direction is found in a study commissioned by the U.S. Treasury Department.[25] Although the study is vulnerable on several key points, it is as good a starting point as any for an exploration of the economic consequences of foreign direct investment.[26]

The key question that the Treasury study was designed to illuminate was the balance-of-payment effect on the United States of direct investment in overseas manufacturing facilities. A few important figures from that study are reproduced in Table 2. In puzzling over the meaning of the figures, it ought to be pointed out at once that the study is set up in such a way as to avoid making an assumption with respect to a key question — indeed, *the* key question. That question, of course, is whether the U.S. enterprise would have lost its export markets abroad if it had not made the investment.

In the table, the estimates of Model A are based on the assumption that the U.S. investor had a free choice in de-

---

[25] G. C. Hufbauer and F. M. Adler, *Overseas Manufacturing Investment and the Balance of Payments* (Washington: U.S. Treasury Department, 1968).
[26] For a discussion of its limitations, see my *U.S. Controls on Foreign Direct Investment — A Reevaluation* (New York: Financial Executives Research Foundation, 1969), pp. 39–64. Also R. N. Cooper's review in *Journal of Economic Literature*, VII, December 4, 1969, pp. 1208–09.

TABLE 2

Balance-of-Payment Impact on U.S. of $1.00 of Foreign
Direct Investment in Manufacturing
(*Based on Conditions of Early 1960s*)

	In U.S. Dollars					
	Investment in Canada and Europe		Investment in Latin America		Investment in Rest of the World	
	5th year after	10th year after	5th year after	10th year after	5th year after	10th year after
Model A — The "Free Choice" investment: *						
Income, royalties, fees to U.S.	+0.174	+0.227	+0.064	+0.085	+0.133	+0.210
Net replacement of U.S. exports	−1.265	−1.632	− .443	− .591	−1.104	−1.740
Other trade effects	+ .514	+ .661	+ .244	+ .325	+ .273	+ .429
Total effects	− .577	− .744	− .135	− .181	− .698	−1.101
Model B — The "Defensive" investment: *						
Income, royalties, fees to U.S.	+ .174	+ .227	+ .064	+ .085	+ .133	+ .210
Net replacement of U.S. exports	+ .120	+ .156	+ .090	+ .119	− .296	.466
Other trade effects	− .015	− .021	− .047	− .062	+ .042	+ .068
Total effects	+ .279	+ .362	+ .107	+ .142	− .121	− .188
Total sales	3.120	4.029	1.156	1.540	1.596	2.513

* See the text for the differences in the assumptions embodied in the models.

SOURCE: G. C. Hufbauer and F. M. Adler, *Overseas Manufacturing Investment and the Balance of Payments* (Washington: U.S. Treasury Department, 1968), tables 5–1, 5–3, 5–5 and 5–7, pp. 60–63.

ciding whether to serve these overseas markets by means of a local subsidiary. In Model B, that assumption is reversed; there, it is assumed that the export markets of the United States would have been lost whether or not the investment took place. Our own impressions, based on various studies cited earlier,[27] is that the truth lies somewhere between these two extremes: that, with lags of a few years' duration, U.S. parents would characteristically have been obliged to find some way of protecting their export markets, as the initial innovational advantage on which those markets were built was gradually eroded.

What the figures indicate is the overriding importance of the alternative assumptions that are embodied in the two models. Model A produces results generally supportive of the view that foreign direct investment burdens the U.S. balance of payments. Model B, on the other hand, produces results that indicate the opposite. In neither case are the indications overwhelming; modest changes in assumed relationships could easily reverse the sign of many of the key figures in the table. The changes in reality that have occurred since the early 1960s in some instances have been large enough to underline the dangers of taking these relationships very seriously; for instance, the means by which the subsidiaries of U.S. parents are financed today have undergone an enormous change since the time when these data were collected.

As far as balance-of-payment effects are concerned, therefore, the net conclusion to be drawn from the Treasury study is the Scotch verdict: "not proven." The range of results that are offered by the two models is wide enough so that one cannot say where reality lies. Besides, the incomplete as-

---

[27] L. T. Wells, Jr., "Product Innovation and Directions of International Trade" (unpublished D.B.A. thesis, Harvard Business School, 1966) ; R. B. Stobaugh, "The Product Life Cycle, U.S. Exports, and International Investment" (unpublished D.B.A. thesis, Harvard Business School, 1968) .

pects of the model suggest that one can develop a set of plausible estimates which spread over an even wider spectrum. If, for instance, it were assumed that the introduction of the U.S.-owned subsidiary affected productivity levels in the host country, one would have to trace out the consequences of the income changes and the efficiency changes associated with the changes in productivity. And if one were to assume some effects on aggregate demand for U.S.-type products in the host country, the range of estimates would widen further.

Apart from balance-of-payment effects, however, there is also the question of the aggregate returns from such activity to the U.S. economy; and there is the no-less-important question of who shares in the return. In addressing these questions, remember that what the U.S. economy sends abroad each year in actual funds in order to enlarge its direct investment stake is something like $3 billion, and that the stake itself grows annually in an amount that comes to about $10 or $12 billion. Viewed as a reduction in savings available for U.S. investment, the $3 billion sum is not a very impressive figure; it could easily be swamped or offset by routine monetary policies aimed at achieving an adequate supply of internal investment.

In terms of the diversion of domestic resources, the main effects of foreign direct investment probably are to be found in this foreign direct investment's impact on the attention and focus of U.S. top management teams, rather than its impact on more familiar and conventional resources. The attention of top management in an organization undergoing rapid change can be a bottleneck item, one that is not easily expansible in the short and medium term; if the facilities abroad are rapidly being expanded in Taipei, the possibility of refurbishing the plant in Peoria and increasing its efficiency may take slightly lower place in the list of issues considered by the board. The effect of that shift in key managerial attention may be to reduce the prospects for productivity increases in the U.S. part of the multinational establishment from what it might otherwise have been. That shift, if it occurred, could shift the relative rewards generated by the enterprise; without reducing the returns to management or the stockholders, it could conceivably reduce those to labor. Whether a factor of this sort is large or trivial defies serious measurement; my guess is that this factor is marginal in effect.

The diversion of U.S. managerial attention from its U.S.-based facilities to its overseas facilities, however, is not the only consequence of the establishment of overseas facilities. Another consequence, slower and longer run in nature, is an increase in the aggregate management and innovation function performed by the U.S. economy. That increase adds to the opportunities of management-trained personnel and of the related business-service industries — engineering, computer sciences, and so on. In the process, however, the familiar policy problem arises: how to upgrade labor so that it can fill the opportunities generated by the expansion in management-related activities.

Observe that these effects have been discussed without introducing the question of impact in the countries receiving the investment. Because part of that impact could eventually work its way back into the U.S. economy, it can hardly be ignored.

First of all, it seems overwhelmingly likely that the activities of U.S. multinational enterprise abroad add to the rate of growth and productivity of other countries.[28] If that is so,

---

[28] Although hard evidence in support of the conclusion is difficult to find, the conclusion is shared by many researchers. See A. E. Safarian, *Foreign Ownership of Canadian Industry* (Toronto: McGraw-Hill Co. of Canada, 1966) ; J. H. Dunning, "Technology, United States Investment and European Economic Growth," cited earlier; D. T. Brash, *American Investment in Australian Industry* (Cambridge: Harvard University Press, 1966) ; Jacques Gervais, *La France Face aux Investissements Etrangers* (Paris: l'Entreprise

there are numerous effects to be considered. One group of effects operates through the incomes of the countries receiving the investment; the other group through changes in their levels of efficiency.

As a general proposition, countries that are surrounded by well-to-do neighbors tend to prosper; this is one of the oldest clichés in the trade policy business, and one of the most valid. Increased incomes in neighboring countries generate new demands, and these lead to new exports. The trouble is, of course, that since increased incomes also mean increased efficiencies in the country where they develop, some degree of adjustment in the trade patterns of all the countries concerned is generally called for. The policy problem consists of how best to manage the adjustment so that (1) the process itself is relatively painless and equitably shared; and (2) the new equilibrium at the end of the process is the best achievable. The trouble with restrictive approaches to that problem is always the same. Even when they seem to contribute a little to meeting the problems of the transition, they lead the economy toward an equilibrium in which everybody may be worse off than he otherwise would be: management, labor, and the stockholders.

The difficulties in this situation, from the viewpoint of labor's interests, are of three sorts. One is the strong psychological impact that occurs when there is a shift of production from a specific identified plant in the United States to a specific plant abroad; shifts that are less visible and more indirect, even if they are just as sure, are easier to tolerate. The second is the indirectness of the route by which U.S. labor derives its benefits from the operations of the U.S. multinational enterprise. Those benefits, to the extent that they exist, have to be achieved (a) through increases in the well-being of the trading partners of the United States,

Moderne, 1963); Jean-Jacques Servan-Schreiber, *The American Challenge* (New York: Atheneum, 1968).

leading to increased demands on the U.S. economy; and (b) through shifts in the comparative advantage of the United States, leading to higher grade jobs. The third difficulty, perhaps the greatest of all, is labor's perception of its weakened bargaining position as it negotiates with the management of multinational enterprises; the recognition by both parties that management sees itself as having a new locational choice is seen as weakening labor's capacity to negotiate effectively.

Despite those difficulties, however, simple prohibitions on the spread of multinational enterprises are hardly an answer. If not multinational enterprises, then what? The transfer of knowledge that multinational enterprises facilitate would probably occur in any case, albeit with a lag. The import of labor-intensive products into the United States would probably occur as well, unless severe import restrictions were maintained. The effects of such import restrictions and related prohibitions would then have to be measured in terms of the usual variables with which trade theorists are familiar: in terms of higher prices and reduced living standards in the United States and elsewhere. Conceivably, there might be some short-term gain for some unskilled and middle-skill workers of the U.S. labor force. But the living standards and opportunities for their children would almost certainly be reduced.

One final point. The inference to be drawn from this paper should not be misunderstood. There is no implication in this discussion that the regulation of multinational enterprises is inevitably misguided and will inescapably do harm to U.S. interests. The conclusion here is much more modest: that simple restrictions on multinational enterprises designed to change the relative rewards between management, labor and the stockholder run grave risks of misfiring, that they may prove impotent; or, if not, that they end up by reducing the opportunities and rewards for all. This still leaves plenty of room for some public approach to the problems generated

by the multinational enterprise. But that is the subject of
another paper.

VI. Summary

The act of establishing a foreign subsidiary is wholly different in implication from that of making a portfolio investment overseas. It implies much more than the investment
of finance capital; and its implications for the parent are not
fully expressed by the profits that are generated. These subsidiaries tend to be established principally in industries that
are innovative and oligopolistic, principally for the purpose
of exploiting the oligopoly advantage or for the purpose
of protecting a market that previously had been exploited
through exports. The products that lie at the heart of the
so-called "trade problem," such as shoes, textiles, and simple
electronics, are not characteristically the products in which
multinational enterprises specialize. When the U.S. economy assists foreigners in the production of these "problem"
products, the characteristic route is through the sale of machinery, the sale of engineering services, or the provision of
distribution facilities.

The forces that have generated overseas investment by
multinational enterprises are of very long standing, going
back nearly 100 years. The basic oligopolistic strength of
U.S. enterprises has been based on innovations that responded to unique market opportunities in the United States. In
any given product, the oligopoly advantages have tended to
erode over time; U.S. enterprises have tried to prolong their
hold on foreign markets by producing closer to such markets;
and eventually, U.S. enterprises have been forced to share
those markets with foreign imitators. The United States has
managed to hold its foreign trade position mainly by moving
on through innovation to new products, basing these inno-

vations upon the unique characteristics of the U.S. market that they confronted.

In trying to project whether the United States is capable of continuing this process, one confronts conflicting indications. On the one hand, the position of the United States as an innovative leader is stronger than ever. On the other hand, the capacity of others to imitate is greater than ever. The outcome, therefore, is indeterminate. The only thing one can say with certainty is that as products become standardized and as their technology is diffused, the capacity of the United States to hold on to its oligopoly position inevitably declines.

The industrialization of less developed countries brings a new dimension to the situation. Instead of using Europe as the low-wage site for defensive production, U.S. enterprises have begun to use countries such as Mexico, Taiwan, and other less developed areas. Although these areas have often been relatively high-cost areas in the early stages, unit costs have tended to decline as the volume of output has increased and as the learning process in the labor force has advanced.

The less developed world is now well within the planning horizons of U.S. parents. But U.S. markets are also well within the scanning capabilities of other producers in these areas, whether or not they are associated with multinational enterprises.

From an economic point of view, the principal effects of U.S. investment overseas are to be found not so much in the movements of resources across international boundaries as in the mobilization of resources within the host country. Most of the money and most of the labor that are mobilized in connection with these operations are local in character; they are, however, infused with the knowledge and attached to the scanning capabilities and firm — specific knowledge of the multinational parent.

In balance-of-payment terms, the best measurements that have so far been developed support none of the extreme propositions that are commonly advanced with regard to multinational enterprises. They neither support the view that foreign direct investment is hurtful to the U.S. balance of payments, nor the conflicting view that such investment is hurtful to the balance of payments of host countries. They do suggest, however, that multinational enterprises are making some contribution to global welfare; that is to say, that they are adding to the efficiency with which the world's resources are being used.

Who shares in these resources and how much is a little more obscure. Stockholders probably gain something from these investments; management almost certainly does; the economy of the host country probably does, as well. Labor in the United States, on the other hand, must count on getting its benefits by a relatively indirect route: from the stimulus that goes with the increased prosperity of the trading partners of the United States; and from the stimulus that derives through shifts in the comparative advantage of the United States, leading to higher grade jobs. There is an understandable reluctance on the part of labor to accept the short-run problems of adjustment for the long-run opportunities for growth. The difficulties with pursuing any other approach, however, are twofold: first, the adjustment would be forced upon labor in any case, as other countries acquired the knowledge and the resources to move into the areas in which the United States had previously led; and, second, resistance to the shift in comparative advantage would tend to depress U.S. incomes until the existing U.S. lead was eaten away by the failure to upgrade the U.S. job mix.

Although simple restrictions on multinational enterprises run grave risks of misfiring, it does not follow that all regulation of such enterprises is inevitably misguided and harmful. There is plenty of room for some public approach to the problems generated by the multinational enterprise. But that is the subject of another paper (see "Problems and Policies Regarding Multinational Enterprises").

Multinational Enterprise and National Security

(Reprinted from the *Adelphi Papers*, March 1971,
by permission of The Institute for Strategic Studies)

Multinational Enterprise
and National Security

In the past twenty years or so, Americans have been increasing their assets outside the United States faster than those at home. They have been acquiring real estate, securities, bank accounts and going businesses abroad at a rate that has brought the "outside" assets under their control near the $200 billion mark. This aspect of *le défi Américain*, however, has been matched by a countermovement of similar proportions by others. Europeans and Japanese also have been enlarging their holdings outside of their home territories at considerable speed. Their holdings in the United States alone, for instance, have risen to the neighborhood of $100 billion. As far as the developed countries are concerned, therefore, the interests of their nationals now sprawl untidily over the globe.[1]

Developments of that sort are hardly new in human history. It is no new experience for nations to see their national interests extending well beyond their boundaries. Cases in which sovereigns have been called on to protect the overseas interests of their nationals or have put those interests to work in the name of national security are common enough.

---

[1] Some salient figures relating to American-controlled multinational enterprises are presented in the appendix tables. Analogous figures for the multinational enterprises of other countries are not available in quite the same form and detail, but they can be pieced together from a number of different national and international sources.

NOTE: Professor Vernon acknowledges the generous support of the Center for International Affairs at Harvard University in the preparation of this paper.

But today, there are some differences. One such difference is a question of scale: the size and extent of the ownership of overseas assets by nationals has dwarfed anything of the kind previously experienced. Another difference is more profound. The conduit for overseas growth has changed.

Today, the principal medium by which outside assets are built up is the multinational enterprise, that is, the enterprise headquartered at home which maintains operating arms of its home business in foreign locations. The assets that are committed by the nationals of one country in another through a multinational enterprise differ from the assets of the traditional international investment. Those of the multinational enterprise are directed and managed day by day according to some business strategy which links those assets to others all over the globe. This is a large step away from the days when the overseas assets of the advanced countries were represented mainly by pieces of paper issued by governments, railways, and power plants acknowledging the right of the holder eventually to receive some funds from the issuer. In order to understand the implications of this change for national security, it will help to examine some aspects of the nature of multinational enterprises.

Nature of the Multinational Enterprise

For 500 years or more, the sovereign states have occasionally found it useful to create artificial persons; and having created such persons, to endow them with some of the attributes of natural men, including the right to own and owe, the right to sue and be sued, and — *mirabile dictu* — the right to nationality. Entities such as the British East India Company, the Dutch East India Company, the Hudson's Bay Company, and the Massachusetts Bay Colony were familiar examples.

These entities represented an extension of the Crown's personality; they were its instruments and its subjects. And it goes without saying that, like natural persons, they were entitled to call on the Crown for protection as needed.

The modern corporation has descended in an unbroken lineage from these early aberrations. But it has managed to acquire some rather extraordinary attributes along the way.

First, the main restrictions that once limited the powers of the corporations have been shed. Until a century ago, the powers of corporations created in the United States and Britain had characteristically been sharply limited by their charters. They were generally confined to certain explicit economic activities, such as banking or canal-building or trading in certain specified areas; their life-span was usually confined to some given period; and the maximum size they could legally attain was generally specified.

By World War I, however, practically all of these restrictions had gone by the boards, both in the United States and Western Europe. By that time, corporations could be formed by practically anyone for practically any purpose without limit of time or size. More important, however, was the fact that corporations by this time had acquired the extraordinary right to own other corporations. With that right established, all sorts of new possibilities were opened up. An enterprising group pursuing a given business strategy could create a separate corporation to perform each different element of the strategy, thus ensuring that their legal accountability was limited and their financial eggs were not contained in a single basket. If their masters so chose, the separate corporations could be made to respond to a common will, and to provide mutual support. The advantages of separateness and the advantages of agglomeration were brought together in a single institution.

When corporations created in different national jurisdic-

tions were linked together in a single multinational enterprise, the virtues of multiple nationality were added to those
of multiple identity. An American entity that enjoyed all
the rights and privileges for doing business in the United
States could join its resources and relate its strategy with a
British entity in Britain, a French entity in France, and so
on; and the resulting union, while retaining its compart-
mentalized multiple identity, could be made to respond to
a common purpose and to draw on a common pool of resources.

It would be too gross a simplification to say that each national part of a multinational enterprise acquired the same
rights and privileges in the country where it was located as an
enterprise that was locally owned. The labyrinthine legal
doctrines that were applied when national laws were in conflict, for instance, drew heavily at times on such metaphysical
concepts as the location of the "real seat" of an enterprise,
that is, the principal decision-making center.[2] But there were
also more obvious distinctions made by many nation-states
between "our" enterprises and "theirs." Long before World
War II, corporations owned by foreigners, even if created
under local law, were commonly prohibited from engaging
in public broadcasting, in coastwise shipping, in munitions
manufacture and in other "sensitive" industries.[3] Besides,
when the companies concerned were very large in relation

[2] For a recent exploration of this concept, especially as it applies to Europe,
see Eric Stein, "Conflict-of-Laws Rules by Treaty: Recognition of Companies in a Regional Market," *Michigan Law Review*, vol. 68, no. 7, June 1970,
pp. 1327–54.

[3] For summaries of these limitations, see Symposium sponsored by International and Comparative Law Center, Southwestern Legal Foundation, *Rights
and Duties of Private Investors Abroad* (New York: Matthew Bender, 1965) ;
D. F. Vagts, "United States of America's Treatment of Foreign Investment,"
Rutgers Law Review, vol. 17, no. 2, Winter 1963, pp. 374–404; and, by the
same author, "The Corporate Alien: Definitional Questions in Federal Restraints in Foreign Enterprise," *Harvard Law Review*, vol. 74, no. 8, June
1961, pp. 1489–551.

to the economy in which they hoped to do business, it was inevitable that the terms of their entry should be fashioned on an *ad hoc* basis. Accordingly, foreign-owned mining companies, oil companies and large-scale plantation enterprises commonly found it necessary to come to special terms with the host government, involving distinctive rights and distinctive obligations. Still, despite these qualifications, the day-to-day business of foreign-owned subsidiaries was generally conducted around the world on a basis that was not very different from that of locally-owned enterprises.

The experiences of World War II offered a hint that the problem of the nationality of industry might one day arise as a major issue. The question "What is an alien?" which had already arisen in World War I, came back again in stronger form. Should the factories of the German subsidiary of General Electric, located in Germany, be dealt with as if they were owned by a German "national?" And how should the United States classify an American company whose parental links could be traced to a German parent, thence to a Swiss grandparent? To disentangle such issues, the principal allied countries found the need to develop elaborate international agreements which among other things set out some ground rules aimed at defining what was an enemy alien and what not.[4]

While the sovereign states have occasionally found themselves trying to sort out who was whose, the enterprises themselves have not wholly been unaware of some of the advantages of multiple national identity. In wartime, the subsidiaries of foreign-owned enterprises commonly performed their assigned wartime tasks without any overt indication of their foreignness.[5] It was characteristic of such cases that,

[4] Malcolm Mason, "Conflicting Claims to German External Assets," *Georgetown Law Review*, vol. 38, January 1950, pp. 171–99.

[5] For characteristic experiences involving subsidiaries of the Ford Motor Company abroad, see Mira Wilkins and F. E. Hill, *American Business Abroad:*

with a fine indifference to ownership, the local managers put the premises to work for the local war effort, at the same time as bombers carrying the insignia of the parent's government sought diligently to blow them up. In an exceptional case or two, enterprises were also known to try to use their national ambiguity to more explicit advantage, arranging their inter-affiliate relationships so that they could claim to be on the winning side, whatever that side might turn out to be.

Even in situations short of actual warfare, the potentialities of multiple identity have at times proved most attractive. Both Royal Dutch Shell and Unilever, for instance, have carefully developed the dual Dutch-British nationalities of the parent because they have found the ambiguity to be useful. When Sukarno was being beastly to Dutchmen, these enterprises emphasized their British identity. But when someone declares a vendetta against the British, it is the Dutch identity that comes to the fore.

The advantages of ambiguities of this sort have been evident at times not only to the enterprises but also to the governments with which they deal. Governments in power tend to follow a more pragmatic policy at times than the ideology which they publicly profess. Those that are trying to survive in the mercurial politics of the less developed world sometimes want to tap the resources of a large "American" enterprise without being obliged to acknowledge locally that they are doing business with the ideological enemy. In that case, a little protective coloration, transparent though it may be, is still welcome; doing business with an intermediate company, "European" or "Middle Eastern" in apparent identity, is often an acceptable arrangement, even if the company is obviously owned by an American parent.

Ford on Six Continents (Detroit: Wayne State University Press, 1964), pp. 64–87, 311–36. For references to experiences in the U.S. and elsewhere, see D. F. Vagts, "The Corporate Alien," *op. cit.*, pp. 1524 ff.

Despite the fact that the ambiguousness of the identity of multinational enterprises has not been altogether a drawback for host countries, most countries on balance have felt an increasing need to pierce the corporate veil. In addition to laying special restraints on foreign-owned subsidiaries at the time of their entry, therefore, most have tended to distinguish such subsidiaries in the treatment accorded under local law and regulation. In some cases, these distinctions violated treaty obligations to the contrary, treaty obligations that bind each contracting state to grant nondiscriminatory treatment to the local subsidiaries owned by the nationals of the other states. But commitments of that sort were set aside, as various states — impelled mainly by questions of national security or national prestige — strove to reduce the role of foreign-owned subsidiaries in various "key sectors" of the local economy.

Discriminatory treatment has taken many forms. When dispensing research subsidies, for instance, government officials have had a keen eye for the ownership of local enterprises. In view of the national purposes in granting such subsidies, one could hardly have expected the British, the French, or the Japanese, to make such awards impartially; that would mean dispensing research funds not only to the struggling computer companies that are locally owned but also to the local subsidiaries of IBM, GE and Honeywell. Propelled by the same kind of consideration, national governments have developed discriminatory policies in public purchases, in the rationing and subsidizing of local credit, in the admission of foreign technicians and in the screening of corporate mergers and consolidations. Throughout, there has been an attempt to build up locally-owned enterprises at the expense of the foreign-owned contingent.

The United States has not been wholly free of discriminatory practices of this sort. The procurement regulations of the defense agencies have sometimes excluded American corporations whose management or ownership included foreigners. The facilities extended by the United States government to "American" corporations that invested in less developed countries, such as insurance against the losses of expropriation and war, have not been available to "American" corporations that were primarily owned by foreigners. On the whole, the United States government has made less of this sort of distinction than other governments have done. But the lesser use of such practices has been due partly to the fact that the regulatory powers of the American government have been rather less extensive than those of Europe or Japan. Besides, the United States government has tried to make a show of tolerance for foreign-owned subsidiaries in the United States in order to increase the tolerance of foreign governments for American-controlled subsidiaries in their countries.

Despite the restraints and roadblocks, however, the multinational enterprise has become more visible. That increased visibility has raised a variety of questions about its relations to the national defense.

Place of the Multinational Enterprise

A penchant for hyperbole has led many who speculate about the future to see the world dominated a few decades hence by several scores of large multinational enterprises. That outcome, however, is still quite remote.

So far, according to the crude statistics covering American-controlled enterprises, there are about 200 large United States parent companies with heavy overseas commitments in manufacturing and raw materials extraction. These enterprises, taken all together, probably account for about one-third of manufacturing sales in the United States proper. Through their subsidiaries and branches, they cover about 6 or 8 percent of manufacturing sales in the other advanced countries and 10 or 12 percent in the less developed countries. In addition, there are many multinational enterprises headquartered in the other advanced countries — notably companies with headquarters in Britain, Germany, France, Italy, Switzerland, the Netherlands, Sweden, and Japan. These also contribute considerable amounts both to their own national output and to "foreign" output of manufactured goods and raw materials. By a heroic numerical leap, multinational enterprises can be thought of as embracing one-quarter to one-third of the output of goods in their "home countries" and one-sixth or so of the output in countries that are foreign to the parent.[6]

If there are national security problems embedded somewhere in these operations, they lie not so much in the sheer size of the enterprises as in the kinds of activities in which the enterprises specialize.

Take raw materials production. Half a dozen large multinational enterprises are enough to account for three-quarters of the oil that moves in international trade; and a like number would account for about the same proportion of the ores that cross international boundaries to be processed into copper, aluminum, lead, zinc, or nickel. The position of the large enterprises in these industries is most commanding at the unfabricated end of the production chain, where size offers the most obvious advantages; and it is least extensive at the last stages of fabrication and distribution. Still, in all these products, the enterprises concerned operate at all levels, moving the product from one affiliate to the next in a complex chain that reflects an extensive degree of vertical integration.

---

[6] According to some estimates generated by Judd Polk, of the $3,000 billions in goods and services produced annually in the non-Communist world, about $450 billions are produced by enterprises away from their national "home."

In the field of manufactures, the industries in which large multinational enterprises are to be found are principally those in which unique competitive positions — what economists like to call "barriers to entry" — can be built up and maintained through large expenditures. There are two main strategies conducive to this end: those that emphasize the building up of brand names, as in food products, automobiles, and drugs; and those that are based on heavy expenditures in the development of products with unique performance characteristics, as in chemicals and computers. More often than not, the two strategies are found in combination in the same firm.[7]

The propensity of multinational enterprises to concentrate on activities in which entry is difficult means, in effect, that they are heavily represented in the sectors that nations regard as essential to defense. One could go through the familiar drill of reciting the percentages: 40 percent of Britain's computer industry; 40 percent of France's telephone and telegraph industry; 100 percent of Italy's ballbearing industry; and so on. The size of any such figures, however, is arbitrary in some measure, depending on how widely or narrowly one defines an industry.

Whatever the appropriate definition of an industry may be, one is justified in observing that the industries in which multinational enterprises have tended to survive and prosper include those that are prominent in industries producing and processing major raw materials and those that are identified with the forefront of modern industry. These industries occupy a key position in the tense periods before the outbreak of war, to prepare the national economy for

---

[7] The reasons why multinational enterprises are found in industries of the sort described are developed at some length in my "Organization as a Scale Factor in the Growth of Firms," in J. W. Markham and G. F. Papanek (eds.), *Industrial Organization and Economic Development* (Boston: Houghton Mifflin Company, 1970).

hostilities and to signal that state of readiness to the other side. Even where the subsidiaries have been in activities of a more mundane sort, such as food preparations, they have seemed more important in the economy than their simple size indicated, because the marketing strategy of such subsidiaries has demanded an emphasis on distinctiveness.

The operations of the units that make up multinational enterprises have been linked to national security not only because they have tended to cluster in industries that are critical for conventional warfare, but also because they have come to occupy a commanding place in the external transactions of many countries. In a typical year, the United States exports $4 billions or so in the form of direct investment and receives $6 or $7 billions of income from her outstanding direct holdings. In both Britain and the United States, more than a quarter of the exports of manufactured goods consist of transactions between the parents of multinational enterprises and their affiliates. In Latin America, the exports of manufactured goods by foreign-owned subsidiaries, which now well exceed $500 millions annually, probably represent over 40 percent of all such exports from the area.[8] As for exports of raw materials by multinational enterprises, these occupy an overwhelming position in the external transactions of some less developed countries. Saudi Arabia, Iran, Iraq, Libya, Chile, and Venezuela are heavily reliant on the continuation of a flow of raw materials from local facilities managed by foreign interests to the overseas affiliates of those same interests. Although there are many things that nations can do without, if necessary, for their national security, foreign exchange is not usually one of them; in the short run, there is almost no substitute for the foreign exchange earnings that exports generate.

The heavy reliance of some countries upon the operations

---

[8] *Survey of Current Business*, October 1970, p. 20.

of multinational enterprises in the generation and maintenance of a reasonable balance-of-payment position is a symp-
tom of a much larger problem. For the past ten years or so,
international trade and investment have been growing faster
than national trade and investment. If multinational enterprises were abolished tomorrow, the odds are that the higher
rate of growth in international trade and payments would
still continue, albeit in other forms. Measured in gross quan-
tity terms, therefore, most nations are becoming somewhat
more vulnerable to external influences.

If multinational enterprises were abolished, however,
there would be one difference. Transactions between two
affiliates in a multinational enterprise system located in different countries are rather less easily reached by the regulatory devices of a national government than transactions
that are undertaken at arm's length between unrelated parties. Although all businesses in the government's jurisdiction
could be mobilized for war, whether the businesses were
national or multinational, the capacity of the multinational
enterprises to make choices among the prospective belliger-
ents in the prewar disposition of men, money, and materials
are thought to be far greater than that of the nationals. Accordingly, nations that feel a sense of vulnerability to outside
forces as a result of a high level of foreign transactions have
that feeling heightened when the transactions are "internal"
to the multinational enterprise; and heightened still further
when the parent of the enterprise is located on foreign soil.

Multinationals as National Contributors

Whether or not multinational enterprises pose a challenge
at the borders of a nation's territory, the fact remains that
they are capable of making useful contributions to national

growth and national well-being. In the national security context, one of the more obvious contributions is in the production of *matériel* for the national military establishment. Two questions are raised by that fact: does a country increase its ability to generate defense goods by encouraging the establishment of multinational enterprises in its economy; and, if so, does the country's capacity to produce defense goods through the units of multinational enterprises add anything on balance to its defense?

The treatment of these questions requires a certain intellectual diffidence. One is being asked to compare what actually has transpired with what might have occurred if the complex world had been a different place. Would Germany have been more formidable as an industrial power if she had been less willing to accept the subsidiaries of American enterprises; or France and Japan more formidable if they had been more willing? Are the Soviet Union and China handicapped by the absence of multinational enterprises? And are Argentina and Brazil more capable of defending their interests because they have admitted many subsidiaries of foreign-owned enterprises?

A few propositions are quite clear. The capacity to produce goods for defense turns heavily on the ability to scan the technology of the world's producers. That scanning can be done in many different ways: by repatriating a few hundred key scientists from the United States and Europe and putting them to work, as China did in the 1950s; by creating licensing links between local firms and foreign enterprises, as Japan and others have done, and using those links not merely to divide up markets but also to secure and exploit information; by appropriating the technology that can be found in scientific periodicals and patent applications or that can be acquired by industrial espionage, as many countries almost certainly do; and, finally, by permitting or encouraging the creation of subsidiaries of multinational en-

terprises on one's territory, especially enterprises that have
some explicit bearing on defense production.

All of these techniques have costs. All of them can "work,"
in the sense that they can yield information that is more
valuable than the national resources used in securing the information; some of them can work remarkably well.[9] In
terms of efficiency of communication, however, there is a
strong case to be made that detailed industrial information
and ways of producing things are more readily transmitted
by way of multinational enterprises than by any of the other
channels of communication suggested earlier. That heroic
conclusion is not in the nature of things; it is rather an empirical generalization, based on patchy observations about
costs and performance,[10] and supported here and there by
rudimentary propositions about relative efficiency in communication networks.[11]

Of course, once a country assigns a given defense task to
a subsidiary of a multinational enterprise located in its country, such as the manufacture and repair of tanks, there is
always a risk that the country's logistical planners may stop
using other channels for scanning outside sources of information that bear on the manufacture and maintenance of
tanks. If one could assume that the multinational enterprise
were reliable as a conduit for such information, the delega-
tion of the task of tank manufacture to a subsidiary of such
an enterprise might be a sensible national decision. But

---

[9] See, for example, G. R. Hall and R. E. Johnson, "Transfers of United States
Aerospace Technology to Japan," in Raymond Vernon (ed.) , *The Technology
Factor in International Trade* (New York: Columbia University Press, 1970) ,
pp. 325–58.

[10] A summary of the available evidence is in Raymond Vernon, *Sovereignty
at Bay: The Multinational Spread of U.S. Enterprises* (New York: Basic
Books, 1971) . This book is one of a series on the multinational enterprise,
financed by a grant of The Ford Foundation to the Harvard Business School.

[11] For more on the subject of communication, together with bibliographical
references, see my article "Organization as a Scale Factor in the Growth of
Firms," *op. cit.*

what if the central management of the enterprise decided systematically to refrain from passing on to its subsidiary certain types of information that were available to the enterprise? Something like this sort of concern, no doubt, troubles the logistical planner of all countries where subsidiaries of multinational enterprises are important producers. It may very well be that there are hard grounds for the concern. But the dimensions of the problem ought to be very clear.

If the wanted information was proprietary information belonging to the multinational enterprise itself, and if the central management of the enterprise was unwilling to provide it to a subsidiary, there is a presumption that the central management will be unwilling to impart the wanted information by any other route. Given the general preference of multinational enterprises to keep their technology under their control as long as it has considerable proprietary value, the assumption is that more will be communicated inside a multinational system than by way of arm's-length licensing. The area that national authorities would have to concern themselves about, therefore, was the area of technology that a local facility would have access to if it were not a member of the multinational enterprise. This includes information in the public domain outside the country, or information that could be extracted by espionage from the outside affiliates of the multinational enterprise.   *152696*

The problem just described cannot be shrugged off. In mitigation of the problem, however, it is worth noting that various studies of the internal structure of American-based multinational enterprises suggest that the barriers to information inside such enterprises are growing less watertight, not more.[12] Most multinational enterprises have been push-

---

[12] The most extensive study to date of the organizational side of multinational enterprises will appear in a book by J. M. Stopford and L. T. Wells, Jr., shortly to be published by Basic Books as part of the Harvard study of multinational enterprises.

ing their organizational structures in directions that are aimed at facilitating the inside flow of technical information among constituent units in different countries. As the "foreign" side of the activities of these enterprises has grown, that aspect of the business has been incorporated more and more intimately into the mainstream of the enterprise. The compartmentalizing of useful information on tight geographical lines within the enterprise is becoming less possible.

Today, therefore, information travels more effortlessly across boundaries than ever before. Capital installations, such as chemical process plants, are characteristically designed and constructed by multinational enterprises for multinational enterprises; the construction entity scans the world for ideas and designs, while the using entity applies the results wherever its installation may be. Automobile manufacturers adopt techniques where they find them, moving the needed skills from one market to another; they borrow the latest wrinkles for machining aluminum from the subsidiary with the largest experience, and spread it quickly to the others; or they call upon their multinational suppliers of parts to carry the needed skills across national boundaries as the occasion arises. National authorities that rely on the subsidiaries of multinational enterprises for critical technological inputs still need to be sure that the enterprises are receiving what the rest of the system knows and are doing an adequate job of scouring other outside sources. But the authorities also have to maintain that kind of vigilance when they make use of locally-owned facilities for critical defense purposes.

Of course, once some useful information has been moved across a national boundary inside a country, its availability for the national defense is still not wholly assured. One can picture a foreign-owned subsidiary holding back information that would be useful for defense purposes. It would be hard to test whether anything of the sort has occurred in the past. The sort of casual evidence that can be gleaned from business histories suggests that when a nation is under siege — when it is preparing for war or engaged in actual combat — the information which has been transmitted to the local subsidiary is usually at the service of the state to the same degree as if the ownership of the enterprise were in local hands. In World War I and World War II, as nearly as any outsider can judge, the facilities of National Cash Register and Ford in Germany, for instance, were exploited just as effectively as the nationally-owned facilities of their local competitors.

Although foreign-owned subsidiaries may be no less "reliable" as wartime producers than locally-owned enterprises, there is one possibility that each nation will surely want to explore with care. This is the possibility that the plants of multinational enterprises are geared to dependence on outside products to a greater extent than the plants of locally-owned enterprises. Generalizations on that point are a bit dangerous. So much depends on the industry and the country involved. Insofar as there is evidence on this point covering industry in the large, it suggests that there is not much basis for such a concern. It is clear that the units of multinational enterprises make a much heavier contribution to international trade as a whole than do national entities. But that is due in considerable part to the selection of industries in which multinational enterprises concentrate, such as raw materials processing, automobiles, and chemicals. Industry mix aside, the propensity for foreign-owned subsidiaries to engage in international trade is mainly due to a heavier stress on exports, not to heavier stress on imports. According to the limited data, foreign-owned enterprises have depended only a little more than locally-owned enterprises upon foreign sources when acquiring machinery and intermediate products.[13] And some make the assumption that even this mod-

---

[13] G. C. Hufbauer and F. M. Adler, *Overseas Manufacturing Investment and the Balance of Payments* (Washington: U.S. Treasury Department, 1968), pp. 20–28.

est tendency is to be encouraged because it reflects better market intelligence and leads to higher efficiency.[14]

There is an understandable preference on the part of nations, nevertheless, to keep foreign-owned enterprises out of "sensitive" industries associated with national defense. Nations can accept the support of the foreign-owned enterprises only as long as the efficiency gained by sharing the superior information grid of the enterprise is not offset by other losses. Those losses include not only a fear of reliance on outside sources of materials but also a fear of sharing the information grid with others. Some delicate choices are involved. IBM computers are reluctantly bought and put to work by the defense authorities in other countries for just so long as the substitute "national" product would be substantially inferior; but light submachine guns, ingenious though they may be, can be designed and manufactured by local interests. In this choice, there is always the wistful hope that somehow the foreigner's role can be made less critical or can be dispensed with altogether.

Japan ranks high among the nations that have gone to some lengths to keep foreign-owned industry out of sensitive sectors. The case of Japan is commonly cited for the proposition that such a policy is feasible — that multinational ownership is not important for the efficient transmission of technology, and that the use of licensing can be at least as efficient. But the case of Japan may demonstrate much less. For one hundred years, Japan has doggedly and consistently spent large sums and considerable manpower in an effort to bargain effectively for technology. Her negotiating position has been bolstered by the fact that most of the technology she sought was not very closely held. It has been strengthened also by the fact that Japan's internal market was large, so

---

[14] Sune Carlson, "Some Notes on the Dynamics of International Economic Integration," *Swedish Journal of Economics (Ekonomisk Tidskrift)*, 1970, p. 24.

that access could be used as an effective bargaining counter. Besides, Japan's workforce was literate and disciplined, so it was capable of applying the information it acquired. Finally, prospective licensers in the United States and Europe saw the prospective Japanese licensees as threatening in world markets if they were not tied up with licensing agreements. Conditions of that sort, coming togther in one nation, may well be *sui generis*. In fact, Japan herself may be finding this strategy less effective, as her needs for outside technology reach into the more esoteric and closely held fields of proprietary information, and as her needs for access to the markets of others begin to erode the negotiating edge that her control over market access once provided.

If there is any country that is entitled to harbor some doubts about the national security implications of multinational enterprises, it is the United States. The widening horizons of American enterprises, their increasing disposition to use remote overseas facilities for the manufacture of components and intermediate products, raise questions about the internal sufficiency of the American industrial complex. Does Ford's overseas fabrication of the engine and transmission system for its new little *Pinto* make any difference to American security; does IBM's production of computerized office equipment in Europe matter from this viewpoint? On the whole, these are not very serious questions, in view of the size and diversity of the American industrial establishment. But they are questions that a military planner would reasonably ask.

Once asked, the answers to such questions are obscure. They are obscured by the fact that the dispensation of benefits by multinational enterprises is not "zero-sum." Measured in absolute terms, all nations may find their military strength increased by the dispositions of such enterprises. The increased sharing of knowledge across international boundaries may enhance the ability of all nations to build better tanks and guns. Moreover, the fact that some of the nation's facilities form part of a multinational system could mean that the output available for actual warfare would come from a logistical structure that was more widely dispersed, a relevant fact in an era of atomic blackmail or actual atomic warfare.

There is one impact of the growth of multinational enterprises upon defense capabilities, however, that has special significance for the United States. The capacity of the multinational enterprise to increase the manufacturing productivity of a national economy, where that capacity exists, stems from its ability to ingest and apply technical information about products and processes. Although the actual production processes of the multinational enterprise do not always occur on American soil, it is likely that the information-storage center of the enterprise as well as the administrative apparatus for planning, adapting, and controlling the enterprise are located there. In short, the United States is specialized in the management function and its ancillary services. As I read the evidence of industry's role in warfare, organizational capabilities of that sort are more important for the satisfaction of national security needs in emergency situations than are the plants themselves.

Since multinational enterprises probably have somewhat strengthened the military capacity of all the countries in which they operate, when capacity is measured in absolute terms, the aggregate capacity with which an embattled non-Communist coalition would confront a Communist world has probably been increased. (As a corollary, the extension of affiliate multinational enterprises inside the Communist countries probably increases the capacity of those countries to a degree that trade would not.) Within the portions of the non-Communist world where the multinational enterprises have operated, however, it is hard to say which parties have been strengthened more: whether the gains to the United States have exceeded those of Europe or *vice versa,* whether those of Argentina have outdistanced those of Brazil.

So far, the emphasis has been on multinational enterprises engaged in manufacturing. Enterprises that are devoted to the exploitation of raw materials and to their processing and distribution are thought to have a quite distinctive impact on national security. Oil, of course, is the outstanding case; but copper, aluminum, iron ore, and others are also involved. In these cases, the operations of the multinational enterprise are tied to national security by two rather different causal chains.

There is one line of wistful speculation that sees international peace as being related to a satisfactory rate of national economic growth, especially the economic growth in the less developed nations. Countries that are growing well, according to this view, are less likely to be a cause of difficulties than those that are not. If the operations of multinational enterprises increase the output of oil and ores from remote places, as they almost certainly do, then the multinational enterprises are the agents of stability through growth. Unless their very presence is an irritant, their contribution to the growth of such places may reduce the areas of troubled waters in which national dissidents or outside revolutionaries may be tempted to fish.

The assumption that economic growth reduces the peace-disturbing propensities of the less developed areas, however, is a doubtful proposition. If there is any relationship between the growth of less developed areas and their contribution to peace among nations, it is very complex. Nations that have never known much growth and that are living near subsistence levels, such as Burma, Mauritania and Paraguay, are rarely heard from. Those that have grown for a time and then had their growth arrested, such as Egypt and Algeria, can be stormy petrels. Yet those that are growing rapidly, such as Libya, are no less capable of contributing to the world's tensions; indeed Libya's very growth is a basis for her capacity to disturb the peace. The underlying relationships between growth and tension in the less developed countries, if relationships exist, have yet to be well understood.

If multinational raw material producers cannot claim to contribute to the defense interests of nations by reducing the number of trouble spots on the globe, they can claim another tie to the defense interests of some of the nations in which they operate. The logistical grid of these enterprises is spread very wide; it draws on many sources and serves many markets. Diversity represents an important form of insurance both to selling and buying nations. It reduces the probability that games of national blackmail will succeed: either blackmail by governments that hold the markets, or blackmail by governments that hold the supplies. (Blackmail by those that control the multinational enterprises is also a possibility, of course; but that is a subject for discussion below.)

Of course, if one could picture a genuinely competitive international market in oils and metals as a real alternative to the present oligopolistic structure, the existence of such a market might represent even a greater measure of insurance through diversity. If the present oligopolistic structure in products of this sort were to weaken, however, it is improbable that big national buyers and sellers would be content to take their chances in an open competitive market. Though such a market reduces the commitment of any buyer to a given source and of any seller to a given market, it introduces the usual uncertainties of price and delivery that are associated with relying on an open market.

The likely alternative to the present oligopolistic structure is a set of relatively inflexible bilateral flows between major producers and major consumers, such as Japan has negotiated in iron ore, copper, and coal. For instance, if the present international network in crude oil were to be eroded, and if industrial users of crude oil were to be cut off from control of their raw materials, both buyers and sellers would be under strong compulsion to recapture some of the stability they had previously enjoyed. One could picture the national oil companies of Iran, Kuwait, Libya, and so on, searching diligently for large-scale importers that were in a position to guarantee a stipulated amount of imports over an agreed time period. More than likely, major refiners and petrochemical producers in the advanced countries would be found that were willing to enter into such contracts *faute de mieux.* However, relations created by such a network of bulk purchase contracts would be much less flexible than the internal logistical arrangements that now exist in the large multinational oil enterprises.

The significance of the multinational enterprise as a form of insurance against national blackmail, however, can easily be exaggerated. As far as the advanced countries are concerned, notably the United States and Western Europe, the power to ward off a blackmail threat, such as the threat of the Arab countries to cut off oil supplies, is probably greater than is popularly supposed.

First of all, comparatively moderate expenditures in the stockpiling of a few key raw materials would reduce such threats to some extent. For instance, one authoritative estimate puts the cost of continuously maintaining a stockpile of six months' oil supply in Western Europe at about 15 percent of the current price of such oil.[15] Fifteen percent may overstate the cost to importing countries, in fact, since the existence of a stockpile in Europe might have the effect of depressing import prices. Ironically, part of what inhibits some public and private organizations from supporting the

---

[15] M. A. Adelman, *The World Petroleum Market 1946–1969* (Washington: Resources for the Future, 1971). Other sources argue in the same direction for the United States, albeit on different facts and assumptions; see Cabinet Task Force on Oil Import Control, *The Oil Import Question* (Washington: U.S. Government Printing Office, 1970). Many industry experts have expressed sharp dissent, but they are not in quite as strong a position to be wholly objective on questions of this sort.

stockpiling step is just that: the fear of lower prices for oil, not the concern for higher prices. The interests of local high-cost oil producers and coal producers combine with those of the multinational enterprises to resist this "solution" to the national defense problem.

The second sense in which the defense problem may be overstated relates to the ability of raw material suppliers actually to hurt the advanced countries even if stockpiles did not exist. That Europe would be hurt by an abrupt interruption in oil supplies goes without saying; but no one has yet made the careful calculations that are needed to determine the size of the problem. Even without data, it is clear that the American case is less difficult. The United States would encounter no more than transitional difficulty if her oil imports were badly interrupted.

In metallic ores, the problem for the advanced countries is even less serious. In this area, the amount of metal that could be saved by postponing the production of consumer-related hardgoods, automobiles, and capital equipment would more than fill any conceivable defense needs.

For all that, the increased sense of psychic comfort that the sourcing patterns of the multinational enterprises provide for the advanced countries is not to be dismissed as a political force.

Multinationals as National Challengers

In a discussion of national security interests, it is hard to know where the limits ought to be drawn; in one way or another, directly or indirectly, any aspect of national life can be said to bear on the question of security.

Still, there is no gainsaying that institutions which threaten to be chronic irritants in relations between the states have some bearing on the national security. It is unnecessary to document the point that the operations of foreign-owned enterprises are a repeated source of irritation to the countries in which they operate.[16]

It also seems fairly evident that there is something systematic in the quality and level of such irritation: that American-controlled multinational enterprises, for instance, tend to generate higher levels of tension in host countries than enterprises controlled from Germany, and the Germans higher levels than the Dutch; that the French and the Japanese find such foreign operations less tolerable in their home territory than do the British and the Belgians; that less developed countries as a whole find the presence (as well as the absence) of such enterprises more nerve-provoking than do the advanced countries; that large enterprises stir more passions than small; and raw material producers more passions than manufacturers.

Elsewhere, I have tried to describe the sources of these tensions and to analyze their causes. In their present context, it is sufficient to concentrate on only one or two of the factors that contribute to the tension-begetting quality of the multinational enterprise.

One element of tension derives from the fact that foreign-owned enterprises are generally seen as outsiders — worse still, outsiders that bring something to the country which the country cannot readily provide for itself: capital or technical capabilities or markets. Even the Swedes are not invulnerable. "Those damned Swedes," says a Canary Islands' expatriate revolutionary, "they own all the hotels, the travel agencies, the buses and the night clubs. And all the stores are run by Hindus. They are the first ones we are going to get rid of." [17]

---

[16] This analysis is developed at much greater length in my *Sovereignty at Bay, op. cit.*, especially chapters 2 and 6.

[17] Quoted in Sanche de Gramont, "Our Other Man in Algiers," *New York Times Magazine*, 1 November 1970, p. 128.

The sense of dependence on the part of the host government may be tolerable as long as the foreigner's role is seen as complementary to domestic interests, rather than competitive. But whatever the starting position of the foreign-owned enterprise may be, some aspects of its existence eventually are seen by local elements as more competitive than complementary. Government officials who originally felt their position strengthened by having brought the foreign investor to their shores eventually feel their position weakened by being closely identified with foreign interests. Local businessmen who once thought of the foreign-owned enterprise as an attractive customer, a reliable supplier, or a beneficent senior partner, eventually develop the ambition to take over the foreigner's interests completely. The timing of these shifts in attitude varies according to country and culture, and according to quirks of personality and style. But it also depends on more systematic factors, such as the dispensability of the capital or technology or markets provided by the foreigners, as judged through the eyes of the local interests.

Some foreign-owned enterprises, therefore, are less vulnerable than others, especially if they are in a position constantly to bolster their negotiating position by generating expectations in the host country of added capital, technology, or markets which the host country could not provide for itself. The pronounced differences in the seeming vulnerability of the international copper companies as compared with, say, the international aluminum companies, can be attributed to just this factor: as seen by host governments, the copper companies no longer have much to offer in the way of capital, technology, or market access, whereas the aluminum companies appear indispensable for the time being.

In most countries, independent intellectual groups — especially groups that are in a position openly to play the role of the political or ideological opposition — are almost certain to be aligned against the foreign-owned subsidiaries. As part of the opposition, intellectuals tend to see the foreign-owned enterprises as allies of the government in power, yet as allies that constitute the government's Achilles' heel. But the opposition of intellectuals is also based commonly on ideological differences that transcend the political strategies of the moment.[18]

What all these groups share in their reaction to multinational enterprises, however, is a common frustration over the relative strength and flexibility of such enterprises, especially in situations in which the interests of the nation and those of the enterprise are clearly at odds. The strength of the enterprise, as seen through the eyes of local interests, lies in the fact that it operates in many jurisdictions. Accordingly, the enterprise is thought able to shift its locus of activities to a more friendly environment whenever the natives seem hostile.

The local concern over the strength and flexibility of multinational enterprises is not wholly hypothetical. When the Mexicans were being difficult in their negotiations with the foreign-owned oil companies in the 1920s and 1930s, the production of Mexican oil by foreign companies fell precipitously — while the production in more friendly Venezuela nearby was growing at a satisfactory rate. When Mossadegh took over the foreign-owned oil properties in Iran in 1952 and when Ovando repeated the Mossadegh performance in Bolivia in 1969, the oil companies suffered less than the countries that had taken the action; and, in the end, the countries were obliged to come to terms with the foreigners.

Concern over the relative strength and flexibility of multinational enterprises is not confined to oil, and it is not limited

---

[18] This is especially true in Chile, for example, where the opposition to multinational enterprises is based in part on a well-elaborated neo-Leninist view that such enterprises create a relationship of "dependence" between Chile and the more advanced countries, especially the United States.

to the less developed countries. American labor complains that the adversary it confronts across the bargaining table is capable of responding to labor's bargaining demands simply by shifting its production to another country — to Taiwan or Mexico or Canada. The French government is frustrated by the fact that if it lays down harsh terms for licensing a General Motors production facility in Strasbourg, the company can do about as well by setting up a facility in Brussels. The perceived flexibility of the enterprise in adversary situations is a source of the deepest uneasiness for the governments through which it must deal.

Underlying all these reactions — governmental, entrepreneurial, intellectual — is a cultural dimension as well, a dimension that has to be invoked in order to understand the differences in the intensity of the response to multinational enterprises that are found from country to country. The French and Japanese uneasiness from the presence of foreign enterprises stands in contrast to the relatively relaxed (though by no means wholly comfortable) reactions of the British and Germans. The ability of the Ivory Coast to embrace the presence of French companies is not to be construed as evidence of an equal tolerance for German or American enterprises. But even if the cultural dimension were absent, the problem would still remain.

All this adds up to the fact that multinational enterprises can be an irritant — at times, even more than an irritant — in international relations. The very importance of the enterprises to the countries in which they operate adds to their tension-generating capabilities. As long as the importance of an enterprise is perceived by interests in the host country as being very large, the tension may not lead to aggressive action. Such action may occur, however, when the country's need for the foreign-owned enterprise begins to decline, ruffling the waters of international relations.

Multinationals as Trojan Horses

The most threatening aspect of multinational enterprises by far — the aspect that links the existence of such enterprises intimately to questions of national defense — is the potential role of these enterprises as the agent of foreign governments. Perhaps it is this factor more than any other that explains why host countries are less uneasy about the presence of subsidiaries controlled by Dutch or Swiss parents than of subsidiaries controlled by American or Japanese parents.

The propensity of national enterprises to work in concert with their governments when operating on foreign soil varies greatly from one country to the next. On the one hand, it would be almost inconceivable for a large French enterprise to take any major strategic move abroad without consulting its tutelary ministry in some depth. In similar vein, no large Japanese enterprise could contemplate an overseas adventure of any significance without substantial consultation with the Japanese Ministry of International Trade and Industry and the Bank of Japan. Even if a formal licensing system did not apply in these countries, the consultation would take place in the ordinary course.

By comparison with other large industrial countries, the United States government exerts comparatively little influence over its enterprises in connection with the operation of its overseas activities. The propensity to avoid *ad hoc* relations with enterprises runs very deep in American law and administrative practice. The usual relationship with such enterprises is arm's length and nondiscriminatory. When the American government has attempted to deviate from that general approach, powerful internal forces have generally arisen to push the relationship back to its customary nonselective patterns. The application of the American system of capital export controls in the 1960s, for instance, began almost on a case-by-case basis; but after some months of operation, it has already reverted to the relatively nonselective and nondiscriminatory approach that is characteristic of American governmental administration.

To be sure, the American government is quite capable at times of working abroad through chosen instruments. Industries such as the petroleum industry and the commercial airlines consist of a sufficiently small number of firms and are associated with sufficiently vital interests that the chosen instrument role is sometimes inevitable. In the case of oil, any interruption in foreign supplies is likely to be followed by hurried consultations between the companies and the key government departments. In the case of the airlines, the chosen instrument approach is bolstered and even made necessary by the international system for the allocation of landing rights. Despite exceptions of this sort, however, the generalization holds.[19]

Although the United States government does not generally have the faculty for close concertment with its overseas enterprises, other countries can hardly be expected to dismiss their fear of Trojan horses from the United States. Even if the behavior of General Motors or Jersey Standard is only occasionally influenced by the suggestions of the American government, the consequences of that influence can be more substantial than a fierce and purposeful thrust on the part of the British government through British Leyland Motors, or by the Italian government through ENI. Besides, the reserve power of the United States economy behind its selected agent, however large or small that agent may be, seems awesome in its potential force from the viewpoint of the countries being acted upon.

---

[19] This conclusion is, of course, less than universally shared. For a contrary view, well reasoned and carefully documented, see Ralph Miliband, *The State in Capitalist Society* (New York: Basic Books, 1970), pp. 28–59 ff. See also W. A. Williams, *The Roots of the Modern American Empire* (New York: Random House, 1969).

Since foreign nations commonly take it for granted that large American enterprises are in some sense the agents (or the masters) of the United States government, they tend to assume also that the enterprises will be protected by their government. That expectation is bolstered by recollections of the Marine landings in Mexico and Central America during the second and third decades of this century, and by the unending promotional efforts of the United States governmental apparatus in favor of "free private competitive enterprise."

From time to time, the United States has demonstrated that the concern of other countries is not totally without substance, even in the current era. Britain, for example, is prevented from selling aircraft to the government of China because the American government refuses to permit an American parent company to send some indispensable electronic components to its subsidiary in Britain; in that case, a British corporation, created under British law, is prevented by the United States from being responsive to British national policy. Perhaps even more egregious was the case of the IBM computer, involving the government of France. In this instance, the United States government came to the conclusion that, as a signatory to the nuclear nonproliferation treaty (NPT) it could not permit the parent American enterprise to send computers to its subsidiary in France, because the instruments would have been used in the operation of a nuclear reactor not subject to the Treaty's control. Although the number of publicized cases in which the United States government has exercised its power in this way comes to only a dozen or two over the past decade, there is no doubt that instances of this sort have been much more common.

The critical question here is not whether the United States was within her rights in these cases but whether other governments felt greatly threatened by the actions. As they saw it, the relationship between, say, IBM in France and its

American parent demonstrated the unwisdom, if not the out-right danger, of relying on the subsidiaries of American-controlled enterprises. Even though the United States was a signatory to the NPT, France was not. The IBM preemption of the field, including the French market, was seen as the moving cause of French vulnerability. If the computer manufacturer in France had been an independent entity, capable of scanning the world for its components and designs, it might conceivably have produced an inferior computer. But it might also have adopted a technology and a sourcing pattern that kept France free of the potential influence of the American government. This case, in short, has been taken as concrete evidence for the fact that the multinational enterprise could undermine rather than contribute to the defense of the host country.

The possibility that governments may direct the parents of their multinational enterprises to instruct their overseas subsidiaries to carry out some national objective seems a good deal higher, on its face, for enterprises whose parents are located in certain European countries or in Japan than for those headquartered in the United States. Countries like Australia and Indonesia cannot have failed to feel some internal qualms at the appearance of Japanese ventures in their economies. But the lesser weight of countries such as Japan, rather than their lesser disposition to control, makes their presence appear less threatening than that of the United States.

One small aside, difficult to resist. It should not be supposed that the subsidiaries of multinational enterprises whose parent units are directly owned by governments are more dangerous from the viewpoint of host governments than multinational enterprises that are privately owned. The leading international oil companies of France and Italy are respectively owned by their national governments, and that of Britain has the government as its principal stockholder.

As instruments of national policy, however, these companies probably are no more feared than privately-owned enterprises of the same nationality; nor, in all probability, should they be. In the quixotic twists and turns of human behavior, one finds that the resistant bureaucrat in a publicly-owned enterprise has almost as many ways of fending off directives from government agencies as the bureaucrat in a privately-owned undertaking. The critical dimension, it appears, is not so much the formal nature of the ownership of enterprises; it is rather the complex system of relations between the governmental apparatus and the enterprise apparatus in the economy. Irrespective of patterns of ownership, one can look to the Japanese and the French to maintain the closest control over the operations of their multinational enterprises, while the British and American governments express their authority in much more dilute form.

Multinationals as Hostages

Although the development and growth of multinational enterprises pose some novel problems in terms of national defense, they also resurrect some very familiar problems of defense in slightly altered guise. Among the familiar problems is that of dealing with the potential enemy when the enemy holds hostages. Governments of nations in which the subsidiary units of multinational enterprises are located have been tempted at times to use these units as hostages, to ensure the good behavior of the country in which the parent is based. This is obviously a part of the strategy that Arab guerrillas keep trying to mount in order to separate the United States from Israel and Europe from the United States.

The use and abuse of hostages by adversaries is a subject

that invites analyses of consummate complexity. It makes a considerable difference, for instance, whether only one party holds hostages or whether hostages have been exchanged, whether the number and quality of the hostages are large or small, and whether the threat to the hostages is latent or explicit.

As far as the advanced nations are concerned, the hostages that each holds have tended to grow rapidly since World War II, as economic and political interests have overlapped and intertwined. Meanwhile, as the United States has enlarged her commitments in the less developed world and as Europe has converted its interests from colonial holdings to arm's-length investments, the less developed nations also have increased their supply of hostages.

My judgment is that this development is one of the critical factors which accounts for a new style in the advanced countries on the subject of the protection of overseas investments. The increase in the number of hostages held all over the world reduces the possibility of a net gain for any side in any international conflict. By the end of any such conflict, the loser may have done away with the hostages he held. Clearcut victories, therefore are less likely than they ever have been. This is one reason why the United States, Britain, and France would have difficulty being utterly nasty to one another on the subject of foreign investment. It is also one of the reasons why these advanced countries have been following a relatively restrained and muted policy in the protection of their business interests in less developed countries. Without much protest or demurrer from the United States, Mexico has been able to force the "mexicanization" of American-owned mining companies, Bolivia has nationalized the properties of Gulf Oil, Peru has taken similar steps toward the International Petroleum Company, Chile has nationalized the holdings of the American copper companies and so on. Yet, only in the case of Cuba and only after all the hostages were "destroyed," did the United States unambiguously attempt some punitive action. Britain has reacted in similarly muted measures toward threats and take-overs affecting properties of her nationals in Asia and Africa. France, exposed to like measures in North Africa, has had a similarly restrained response.

However, the reaction of the advanced countries in the protection of their investors' interests in the less developed world might be a good deal more aggressive were it not for some other factors. One of these is the realization that political leaders in the less developed countries often need the form of a successful nationalization much more than they need — or want — its substance. As long as these countries lack capital, technology, or foreign markets, they are disposed to find some means of maintaining some of the substance of their old arrangements if they can, even when they alter its form. Sukarno's handling of the nationalized oil companies in Indonesia during the mid-1960s was a classic illustration of the pattern; so was Bolivia's handling of the Gulf Oil nationalization. To the extent that this factor remains, all parties to the dispute are disposed to conduct it in muted terms.

A third factor that has led the advanced countries to apply caution and restraint in the conduct of these disputes is the increased capacity of the less developed countries to make effective coalitions: coalitions among themselves, or coalitions with the Soviet Union and China. Egypt's handling of her relations with the United States and East Africa's managing of the Tan-Zam Railroad project are illustrative. This capacity for coalition increases the ability of the less developed countries to threaten with credibility. That fact represents a change of far-reaching importance which deeply affects the economic interests of the advanced countries, including the position that their multinational enterprises are likely to play in matters of national security.

Possibilities for the Future

It is a tangled skein that links multinational enterprises to the problems of national security. But a few threads are visible and clear.

There has been a trend toward increased economic interdependence among nations; both the advanced countries and the less developed countries are exposed to that trend, as each reaches outward for more technology, more capital, more labor, more land, and more markets. In the process, multinational enterprises have taken a position of increased importance in international economic relations. While that growth has created difficulties, the lopsided nature of the multinational enterprise phenomenon — the fact that American-based enterprises have been so much more important than the enterprises of other countries — has added to those difficulties.

Although multinational enterprises have maintained or extended their position across international boundaries, however, my guess is that their utility and availability as instruments of national security are declining, not increasing.

Part of the reason for the expectation stems from a key assumption stated earlier, the assumption that the United States and other advanced countries are in a relatively poor position to use very vigorous measures in promoting and defending the interests of their overseas enterprises. If that should prove to be the case, then the multinational enterprises themselves are likely to adapt to the fact. Those adaptations, if they occurred, would reduce even further the utility of such enterprises as instruments of national policy. What kind of adaptation is to be anticipated?

History is filled with incidents that attest to the fact that the principal business of business is business. Attachment to a particular flag may be of great importance to some of the individuals associated with the bureaucracy of a multinational enterprise. But the degree to which that attachment is expressed in policy will depend in part on its business utility. This observation carries no pejorative overtones; it does not distinguish business bureaucracies from any other, certainly not from the bureaucracies of government. One of the most universal characteristics of large bureaucracies is their capacity for developing a collective conviction that the steps needed to keep their institution strong are socially justified and socially desirable.

I anticipate that multinational enterprises will respond to that imperative. They will pursue their natural bent — the creative business of moving ideas, money, people, and goods in increasing volume across international boundaries — secure in the feeling that they are contributing to social welfare. If my projection is right that governments will be more restrained in the support of the activities of these enterprises, the decline in such support will hardly go unobserved in the board rooms of the enterprises themselves. One of the major reasons for maintaining a close identification with the government of the parent unit will thereby be weakened. "The world is my oyster," a self-conscious household slogan in many such enterprises, will be one step closer to genuine enterprise policy.

As a matter of fact, some of the symptoms of such a trend already are in evidence. It is not wholly accidental that the names of some of the world's leading multinational enterprises are being denationalized, that Food Machinery is now FMC, British Petroleum BP, Badische-Analin Soda-Fabrik BASF and so on. To be sure, some enterprises such as Ford and Coca-Cola, probably do not have the option of diluting their national identity. Others, such as those of the French and the Japanese, will find it difficult on cultural grounds even to contemplate the possibility. But it would be unwise to assume that national associations could not be altered, and less wise still to assume that the alteration will not genuinely affect the self-perception of the enterprise itself.

The ability of an enterprise to dilute its national identification with a single country is determined not only by legal and cultural considerations but also by the nature of the business strategy that the enterprise has accepted. In some industries, such as aluminum and computers, the need for a tightly-controlled international strategy on the part of the firm generally leads the parent to place a high value on exercising very close control over its subsidiaries. Enterprises of this sort will be loath to make organizational changes inside the enterprise that weaken the possibilities for central control. For them, therefore, the use of arrangements that introduce ambiguities in the control apparatus, such as the use of joint ventures or licensing agreements, will be difficult. Enterprises whose strategy requires the continuation of central control, therefore, may have real problems in attenuating the national identity of the system to which the subsidiary belongs. It may be that such enterprises will concentrate their efforts on devices of the sort that Unilever and Royal Dutch/Shell have employed, such as the use of dual national identities and similar arrangements. For some in this category, the possibility of regional holding companies as identity buffers will also exist.

Enterprises that do not need very tight central controls, however, are likely to engage in organizational stratagems that generate greater national ambiguity. Entities that do little international cross-hauling and that sell mainly to local markets will find this an attractive possibility. Joint ventures and management contracts will be used by such enterprises to an increasing extent.

As a result of adaptations of this sort, it is to be anticipated that multinational enterprises will be even less available as instruments of national strategy than has heretofore been the case. If that fact should begin to be clear to the governments of the United States and other advanced countries, the disposition of those countries to draw a line between multinational enterprises that are "ours" and multinational enterprises that are "theirs" may well decline. When that occurs, the willingness to entertain a multigovernmental approach to the control of multinational enterprises will grow. Once that door is opened, the position of the multinational enterprise in international relations will be greatly changed, and the relationship between multinational enterprises and national security will become more attenuated than ever.

TABLES

I. DIRECT FOREIGN INVESTMENT (ACCUMULATED ASSETS) BY MAJOR COUNTRIES, END 1966
(book value, in millions of dollars)

	World	US	Britain	France	Germany	Sweden	Canada	Japan
Petroleum	25,942	16,264	4,200	d	200	a	a	a
(LDC)	(11,892)	(6,975)	(2,167)	(670)	(65)	a	a	(222)
Mining and Smelting	5,923	4,135	759	a	100	a	250[b]	a
(LDC)	(2,801)	(1,827)	(298)	(200)[b]	(38)	(65)	(202)	(71)
Manufacturing	36,246	22,050	6,028	a	1,800	a	2,988[b]	a
(LDC)	(8,047)	(4,124)	(1,471)[b]	(1,230)[b]	(645)	(96)	(332)	(270)
Other	21,472	12,113	5,015[c]	a	400	a	a	a
(LDC)	(7,230)	(3,915)	(2,255)	a	(97)	a	a	(33)
Total	89,583	54,462	16,002	4,000[b]	2,500	793	3,238	1,000
(LDC)	(29,970)	(16,841)	(6,184)	(2,100)	(845)	(161)	(534)	(605)

NOTES

Italy, Holland, Switzerland and Belgium data not available; Australian total investment is $300 m.
'LDC' refers to less-developed countries comprising all Latin American, African, Asian and Oceanic countries excluding Australia, New Zealand, and South Africa.
[a] Not available.
[b] Estimate.
[c] Including agricultural investment of $1,022 m. ($864 in LDCs).
[d] Total French oil production estimates at 57·2 million tons in 1966.

Source: The Multinational Corporation in the World Economy (ed.), Sidney Rolfe and Walter Damm.

2. GROWTH OF FOREIGN DIRECT INVESTMENT IN THE US AND OF AMERICAN DIRECT INVESTMENT ABROAD

Country	Direct Investments of Foreign Enterprises in the US by Country of Investing Enterprise (millions of US$)			Foreign Direct Investments by American Enterprises or Subsidiaries of American Enterprises by Area and by Industry[a] (millions of US$)						
	Year			Year			Industry 1969[c]			
	1963[b]	1968[b]	1969[c]	1963[b]	1968[b]	1969[c]	Manufacturing	Petroleum	Mining and smelting	Trade and Other
Canada	2,183	2,659	2,834	13,044	19,535	21,075	9,389	4,359	2,764	4,563
Latin America	112	182	193	8,662	13,101	13,811	4,347	3,722	1,922	3,821
Western Europe	5,491	7,750	8,510	10,340	19,407	21,554	12,225	4,805	72	4,453
EEC	1,728	2,790	3,306	4,490	9,012	10,194	6,340	2,243	17	1,593
Britain	2,265	3,409	3,496	4,172	6,694	7,158	4,555	1,563	2	1,037
Switzerland	825	1,238	1,395	672	1,437	1,606	380	−30	0·5	1,256
Other W. Europe	663	313	313	1,006	2,264	2,596	949	968	52	566
Japan	d	181	176	472	1,050	1,218	639	447	0	131
Southern Dominions[e]	d	d	d	d	3,508	3,854	2,209	836	479	510
Other Asia and other Africa	d	d	d	d	5,652	6,189	820	4,108	399	861
All other areas	158	43	105	7,412[f]	2,731[f]	3,061[f]	0	1,708[f]	0	1,353[f]
Total	7,944	10,815	11,818	40,686	64,983	70,763	29,450	19,985	5,635	15,592

NOTES

[a] 'Direct Investment' is defined as the book value of equity and long term debt of foreign enterprises in which the foreign enterprise holds 25 or more per cent of the equity.

[b] All data revised for 1963 and 1968.

[c] All data preliminary for 1969.

[d] Included in relevant 'all other areas' category.

[e] Southern Dominions include Australia, New Zealand and South Africa.

[f] For the most part refers to investments made in international shipping in Panama and Liberia except for 1963 when Southern Dominions, Other Asia and Other Africa are included.

Source: Survey of Current Business, various issues.

3. GEOGRAPHICAL SPREAD OF 9 US-CONTROLLED MULTINATIONAL ENTERPRISES IN PETROLEUM, 1910–67[a]

Crude Oil Operations	1910	1938	1957	1967
Number of enterprises engaged in such operations	1	7	9	9
Number of countries in which engaged	1	20	22	31
Number of country-operations[b]				
in: Canada	0	1	7	9
Britain and Europe[c]	1	8	9	11
Southern dominions[c]	0	0	0	3
Latin America	0	18	18	28
Other	0	13	29	45
Total country-operations	1	40	63	96

Subsidiaries of All Tupes	1913	1939	1957	1967
Number of subsidiaries by area:				
Canada	1	40	135	220
Britain and Europe[c]	59	202	333	626
Southern dominions[c]	2	10	32	68
Latin America	8	68	202	329
Other	3	31	84	199
Number of subsidiaries by principal function:				
Extraction	3	27	33	60
Manufacturing	16	52	92	279
Sales	36	110	156	289
Other[d]	7	65	208	325
Unknown	11	95	297	489
Total subsidiaries	73	351	786	1,442

NOTES

[a] The US enterprises covered in the table are: Cities Service, Continental, Gulf, Mobil, Philips, Standard Oil of California, Standard Oil of Indiana, Standard Oil (N.J.) and Texaco. These comprise the major US-controlled multinational oil companies.

[b] Crude oil operations are commonly carried on through foreign branches of US companies rather than subsidiaries. Each 'country-operation' in the table represents the presence of one of the enterprises in a country, whether by way of branches or subsidiaries. The figures are subject to larger error than those in the lower half of the Table.

[c] Europe includes Ireland and Turkey. The Southern dominions are: Australia, New Zealand, Rhodesia and South Africa.

[d] Includes 'Holding', 'Research and Development', 'Serving and Entertaining', 'Banking', 'Transportation', and 'Name Protection'.

Source: Harvard Multinational Enterprise Study. For background and methodology of study, see J. W. Vaupel and J. P. Curhan, *The Making of Multinational Enterprise* (Boston: Harvard Business School, 1969), pp. 1–8.

4. GEOGRAPHICAL SPREAD OF 9 US-CONTROLLED MULTINATIONAL ENTERPRISES IN NON-PETROLEUM EXTRACTIVE INDUSTRIES, 1910–67[a]

Non-Petroleum Extractive Operations	1910	1938	1957	1967
Number of enterprises engaged in such operations	3	6	9	9
Number of countries in which engaged	1	13	19	22
Number of country-operations[b] in: Canada	0	1	5	6
Britain and Europe	0	2	2	3
Southern dominions	0	1	5	8
Latin America	3	15	20	25
Other	0	1	2	3
Total country-operations	3	20	34	45
Subsidiaries of All Types	1913	1939	1957	1967
Number of subsidiaries by area:				
Canada	1	9	30	55
Britain and Europe	1	8	16	121
Southern dominions	0	5	17	52
Latin America	4	44	83	119
Other	0	3	29	70
Number of subsidiaries by principal function:				
Extraction	3	32	71	67
Manufacturing	3	13	44	165
Sales	0	1	9	77
Other	0	15	32	65
Unknown	0	8	19	43
Total	6	69	175	417

NOTES

[a] The US enterprises covered in the table are: Alcoa, American Metal Climax, American Smelting and Refining, Anaconda Copper, Engelhard Industries, Kaiser Industries Corporation, Kennecott, Phelps Dodge and Reynolds Metal. These comprise the major US-controlled extractive companies.
[b] For definitions of terms, see Table 3.

Source: Harvard Multinational Enterprise Study.

5. NUMBER OF FOREIGN MANUFACTURING SUBSIDIARIES OF 187 US-CONTROLLED MULTINATIONAL ENTERPRISES, BY AREA, SELECTED YEARS 1901–67

Area	1901	1913	1939	1959	1967
Canada	6	30	169	330	443
Europe and Britain	37	72	335	677	1,438
France	8	12	52	98	223
Germany	10	15	50	97	211
Britain	13	23	128	221	356
Other Europe	6	22	105	261	648
Southern dominions	1	3	69	184	361
Latin America	3	10	114	572	950
Other	0	1	28	128	454
Total	47	116	715	1,891	3,646

Source: J. W. Vaupel and J. P. Curhan, *The Making of Multinational Enterprise* (Boston: Harvard Business School, 1969), chapter 3.

6. FOREIGN INTEREST IN EUROPEAN DOMESTIC DEFENCE INDUSTRIES, BY COUNTRY

Country	Firm	Type	Foreign interest
Belgium	Société Anonyme Belge de Construction Aeronautiques (SABCA)	Aeronautical (General)	1. Marcel Dassault (F) 2. VFW-Fokker (Neth, Ger)
France	Société Nationale d'Etude et de Construction de Moteurs d'Aviation (SNECMA)	Aeronatuical (Engines)	1. Pratt & Whitney (US) 10%
Germany	Messerschmitt-Bölkow-Blohm (MBB)	Aeronautical (General)	1. Boeing (US) 9·7% 2. Aérospatiale (F) 9·7%
	Vereinigte Flugtechnische Werke (VFW)	Aeronautical (General)	United Aircraft Corp (US) 26·4%
Italy	Aernautica Macchi	Aeronautical (General)	Lockheed (US) 20%
	Contraves Italiana	Missiles	Oerlikon (Swiss) associate
Netherlands	Fokker	Aeronautical (General)	Northrop Corp (US) 20%
Spain	Construcciones Aeronauticas (CASA)	Aeronautical (General)	Northrop Corp (US) 24%
	La Hispano-Aviación	Aeronautical (General)	MBB (Ger) 27%

7. LARGE FOREIGN MANUFACTURING ENTERPRISES IN SELECTED COUNTRIES

A *Industrial Countries*

i—Foreign Affiliated Enterprises in Japan[a]

Position in Main Industries, 1969		
	% share in total Japanese industries[b]	
Industry	Numerical	Sales
All manufacturing	0·27	3·31
Food processing	0·11	0·74
Chemical manufacturing	3·06	4·06
Pharmaceuticals	2·38	4·87
Petroleum	2·07	60·14
Rubber products	0·72	18·77
Non-Ferrous metals	0·78	5·28
Non-Electric Machinery	0·65	6·65
Electric Machinery	0·50	2·94

NOTES

[a] All enterprises with more than 25 per cent of the equity owned by foreign corporations.
[b] All enterprises with capitalization of more than ¥ 1 million.
Source: The Oriental Economist, February, 1969.

---

ii—Foreign Owned Manufacturing Firms in Selected European Countries

GERMANY, 1969 GNP = $150 billion[a]				
Firm	Rank[b]	Industry	Turnover $m.[a]	Foreign Parent or Controlling Company
Deutsche Unilever	14	Foodstuffs	1248·5	Unilever (Neth, UK)
Esso	15	Petroleum	1235	Esso Standard (US)
Adam Open	16	Automotive	1213·5	General Motors (US)
Deutsche Shell	18	Petroleum	1095·5	Royal Dutch Shell (UK, Neth)
Ford-Werke	21	Automotive	971	Ford (US)
BP Benzin and Petroleum	23	Petroleum	769	BP (UK)
IBM Deutschland	24	Electronics	641	IBM (US)
Deutsche Erdöl	26	Petroleum	630	Texaco (US)
British American Tobacco	28	Tobacco	559	BAT (UK)

NOTES

[a] Exchange rate at DM4 = $1 (first half 1969 rate) .
[b] Rank is according to the turnover of the 30 largest manufacturing enterprises.

(Table 7A (ii) *cont.*)

FRANCE, 1969 GNP = $140 billion[a]				
Firm	Rank[b]	Industry	Turnover $m.[a]	Foreign Parent or Controlling Company
Esso	11	Petroleum	919·3	Standard Oil (US)
Shell Française	12	Petroleum	824·5	Royal Dutch Shell (UK, Neth)
Pétroles BP	15	Petroleum	782·9	BP (UK)
IBM France	19	Electronics	584·5	IBM (US)
Cie Française Philips	21	Elect. equip.	464·7	Philips (Neth)
SIMCA	22	Automotive	454·0	Chrysler (US)
FFSA	23	Automotive	379·5	Fiat (It)

NOTES

[a] Exchange rate at 5·5 francs = $1 (1970 rate).
[b] Rank is according to the turnover of the 30 largest manufacturing enterprises.

BRITAIN, 1969 GNP = $109 billion[a]				
Firm	Rank[b]	Industry	Turnover $m.[a]	Foreign Parent or Controlling Company
Esso	10	Petroleum	1250·4	Esso Standard (US)
Ford	11	Automotive	1171·2	Ford Motor Co. (US)
Gallahers	16	Tobacco	979·2	American Tobacco (US)
F. W. Woolworth	24	Retail trade	710·4	F. W. Woolworth (US)

NOTES

Shell Transport Company (turnover: $5215·2 m.) and Unilever (turnover: $2518·2 m.), which rank 1 and 5 respectively, are British components of Anglo-Dutch conglomerates and therefore not included as foreign-owned firms.
[a] Exchange rate at $2·40 = £1.
[b] Rank is according to the turnover of the 30 largest manufacturing enterprises.

			ITALY, 1969 GNP = $82·3 billion[a]	

Firm	Rank[b]	Industry	Turnover $m.[a]	Foreign Parent or Controlling Company
Esso Italiana	4	Petroleum	973	Esso Standard (US)
Shell Italiana	6	Petroleum	674	Royal Dutch Shell (Neth, UK)
BP Italiana	9	Petroleum	354	BP (UK)
Total	11	Petroleum	297	Cie Française des Pétroles (F)
Mobil Italiana	12	Petroleum	280	Socony Mobil (US)
IBM Italia	16	Electronics	226·5	IBM (US)
Chevron Italia	17	Petroleum	198	Chevron (US)
Philips	26	Elect. equip.	146·5	Philips (Neth)
Rhodiatoce	29	Textiles	142	Rhône-Poulenc (F)
Ignis	30	Elect. equip.	136	Philips (Neth)

NOTES

[a] Exchange rate at 625 lire = $1.

[b] Rank is according to the turnover of the 30 largest manufacturing enterprises.

Source: Business Europe.

(Table 7 *cont.*)

B *Developing Countries*

i—Selected Latin American Countries (*manufacturing* firms only)

MEXICO, 1967 GNP = $26·74 billion[a]				
Firm	Rank[b]	Industry	Sales[a] $m.	Foreign Parent or Controlling Company
Anderson Clayton	2	Diversified	131·2	Anderson Clayton & Co (US)
Fabricas Automex	3	Automotive	101·8	Chrysler Corp (US)
Celanese Mexicana	6	Synth. fibres	62·5	Celanese (US)
Condumex	10	Metals	36·0	Anaconda (US) and Pirelli (It)
Industria Electrica	13	Elect. equip.	23·5	Westinghouse (US)
Union Carbide Mexico	14	Chemicals	22·9	Union Carbide (US)
Bacardi	15	Beverages	19·2	Bacardi (US)
Kimberly-Clark	16	Paper	18·0	Kimberly-Clark (US)

NOTES

[a] Exchange rate at 12·5 pesos = $1.

[b] Rank according to value of sales of 20 largest manufacturing enterprises.

			Total Assets[a]	
Firm	Rank[b]	Industry	$m.	Foreign Parent or Controlling Company

BRAZIL, 1969
GNP = $22·9 billion[a]

Firm	Rank[b]	Industry	Total Assets[a] $m.	Foreign Parent or Controlling Company
Usiminas Siderúgicas de Minais Gerais (USIMINAS)	3	Metals	328·9	Usiminas Nippon KK (Japan)
Volkswagen do Brasil	7	Automotive	214·1	VW (Ger)
Ford-Willys do Brasil	8	Automotive	204·0	Ford Company (US)
Rhodia	9	Textiles	198·0	Rhône-Poulenc (F)
Pirelli	10	Rubber goods	171·1	Pirelli (It)
Ciá Cigarros Souza Cruz	11	Tobacco	154·4	British American Tobacco Co (UK)
Esso Brasileira	12	Petroleum	142·5	Standard Oil of N.J. (US)
Sanbra	13	Foodstuffs	126·5	Bunge y Born (Arg)
Ciá Geral de Motores	14	Automotive	114·0	General Motors (US)
Mercedes-Benz do Brasil	15	Automotive	112·1	Daimler-Benz (Ger)
Shell Brasil	16	Petroleum	109·5	Royal Dutch Shell (UK, Neth)
Geral Electric	17	Elect. equip.	109·0	GE (US)
Ciá Sid. Belgo-Mineiro	18	Metals	92·2	ARBED (Lux)

NOTES

[a] Exchange rate of 4·025Cr. = $1 (October, 1969).
[b] Rank according to total assets of 20 largest manufacturing enterprises.

(Table 7B (i) *cont.*)

ARGENTINA, 1967 GNP = $14·9 billion[a]				
Firm	Rank[b]	Industry	Sales $m.[a]	Foreign Parent or Controlling Company
IKA Renault	1	Automotive	116·0	Regie Renault (F)—38% American Motors (US)— 4% Kaiser Jeep (US)—3%
Industrias Pirelli	5	Rubber prod.	44·7	Pirelli (It)
Tabacos Particulares	8	Tobacco	33·8	Reemtsma (Ger)[c]
Cristolarias Rigolleau	21	Glass	15·6	Corning Glass (US)
Electroclor	24	Chemicals	13·6	ICI (UK)[d]
Sniafa	25	Synth. fibres	13·6	Snia Viscosa (It)
Atanor	29	Chemicals	11·9	Dow Chemicals (US)

NOTES

[a] Exchange rate at 350 pesos = $1 (pre-1970 rate).
[b] Rank according to value of sales of 30 largest manufacturing enterprises.
[c] Through Imparciales in which Reemtsma has a 49 per cent holding.
[d] Through Duperial, ICI's Argentina subsidiary.

Source: Business Latin America.

B *Developing Countries*

ii—Selected Asian Countries (*manufacturing* firms only)

INDIA, 1968–69					
GNP = $42 billion[a]					
Firm	Rank[b]	Industry	Net Assets[a] $m.	Sales[a] $m.	Foreign Parent or Controlling Company
Oil India	5	Petroleum	116·0	34·8	Burmah (UK)
Hindustan Aluminium	8	Metals	74·1	34·8	Kaiser (US)
India Aluminium	9	Metals	64·4	27·1	Alcan (Canada)
Imperial Tobacco of India	10	Tobacco	62·0	76·3	Imperial Tobacco (UK)
Voltas	11	Engineering	50·0	80·7	12% UK and Swiss
Indian Explosives	12	Chemicals	49·3	18·5	ICI (UK)—minority
E.I.D. Parry	13	Chemicals	47·3	37·8	E.I.D. Parry (UK)
Dunlop Rubber	14	Rubber prod.	46·1	74·1	Dunlop (UK)
Union Carbide India	15	Chemicals	44·5	40·1	Union Carbide (US)
Guest, Keen, Williams	16	Engineering	44·0	39·0	GKN (UK)
Hindustan Lever	18	Foodstuffs	41·3	115·3	Unilever (Neth, UK)
Esso Standard Refinery	20	Petroleum	39·3	45·1	Standard Oil (US)
Premier Autos	22	Automotive	37·6	35·7	Fiat (It)—minority

NOTES

[a] Exchange rate at 7·5 rupees = $1.

[b] Rank according to net assets of 22 largest manufacturing enterprises.

(Table 7B (ii) *cont.*)

Firm	Rank[b]	Industry	Sales[a] $m.	Foreign Parent or Controlling Company
		PAKISTAN, 1969 GNP = $15·55 billion[a]		
Pakistan Tobacco Co.	I	Tobacco	112·0	British American Tobacco (UK)
Pakistan Refinery	4	Petroleum	47·4	Shell (UK, Neth)—15% Burmah (UK)—15% Caltex (US) 12% Esso Standard Eastern (US)—18%
Burmah Eastern	6	Petroleum	44·8	Burmah Oil (UK)
Attcock Oil	7	Petroleum	39·3	Attcock (UK)
Premier Tobacco Ind.	8	Tobacco	29·3	Godfrey Phillips (UK)
Lipton Pakistan	10	Tea	25·8	Lipton (UK)
Esso Pakistan Fertilizers	13	Fertilizers	21·6	Esso Standard Eastern (US)
Brooke Bond Pakistan	16	Tea	21·0	Brooke Bond (UK)
Karnaphuli Paper Mills	17	Paper	17·2	Japanese consortium—13%

NOTES

[a] Exchange rate at 4·8 rupees = $1.
[b] Rank according to sales of twenty largest manufacturing enterprises.

Source: Business Asia.

The Multinational Enterprise: Power Versus Sovereignty

(Reprinted from *Foreign Affairs*, July 1971,
by permission of the Council on Foreign Relations, Inc.)

The Multinational Enterprise: Power Versus Sovereignty

I

The extraordinary spread of U.S. enterprises into foreign countries in the last two decades has produced its inevitable aftermath. Though the multinational enterprise as an economic institution seems capable of adding to the world's aggregate productivity and economic growth, it has generated tensions in foreign countries. As a rule, the tensions are a manifestation of powerful psychic and social needs on the part of élite groups in host countries, including the desire for control and status and the desire to avoid a sense of dependence on outsiders.

There are several unresolved conflicts. Sovereign states have legitimate goals toward which they try to direct the resources under their command. Any unit of a multinational enterprise, when operating in the territory of a sovereign state, responds not only to those goals but also to a flow of commands from outside, including the commands of the parent and the commands of other sovereigns. As long as the potential clash of interests remains unsolved, the constructive economic role of the enterprise will be accompanied by destructive political tensions.

II

What can be done about the potential clash? A useful first

AUTHOR'S NOTE: The major conclusions of this article have been expanded in *Sovereignty at Bay: The Multinational Spread of U.S. Enterprises* (New York: Basic Books, 1971).

step in any prescriptive exercise is to attempt a projection based on the assumption that events will be allowed to run their course, without the conscious intervention of new policies. As far as the future of multinational enterprises is concerned, simple projections seem risky. As tension builds, more Chiles and more Cubas could easily develop. Despite such possibilities, however, there have been some exceedingly strong regularities in the patterns of growth and the patterns of relations between host countries and foreign-owned enterprises.

In modern societies, products have commonly moved through a predictable cycle from birth to senescence. As a consequence, the enterprises dependent on any given product have found their negotiating strength constantly in a state of change, rising for a time in the beginning of the cycle, then declining later on.

When a new industrial product is introduced, at first it is unique, controlled by only a few firms. Eventually, the demand for the product grows, the technology associated with its production is diffused and appropriated, and the specifications defining the product become more standardized. As demand grows, the threat of new entrants into the industry also tends to grow. Established leaders in the industry respond by trying to distinguish their standardized products from those of others; consumers are exhorted to put a tiger in their tank or a lark in their future. Sometimes, using various forms of advertising and minor product differentiation, industry leaders have tried to hang on. At other times, they have sloughed off products as they have lost their distinctive characteristics and have turned to the generation of new products. In industries involving raw materials there also has been a slow diffusion of control.

Despite the changing position of U.S. enterprises in any given product, their aggregate opportunities are unlikely to decline. The extraordinary improvements in international communication and transportation seem destined to continue, accompanied by more Intelsats, Concordes, IBM 370s, and all the other modern instruments for shrinking time and space. It seems likely also that the cost of generating and launching major industrial innovations will continue to grow.

On the other hand, it also seems likely that the rate of adoption of innovations by industrial users and consumers will continue to accelerate, when compared with historic norms. So will the rate of appropriation and imitation on the part of the producers that pursue a follow-the-leader strategy. These tendencies, taken in combination, suggest that multinational enterprises which base their business strategy on an innovational lead will have to plan even more than in the past for the speedy exploitation of any industrial advance over the largest possible market.

There are a few other critical projections that can be assigned a high probability. If the European Community grows larger and more cohesive, as seems likely, there will be a growing tendency for large European-owned enterprises inside the area to think of their market as pan-European rather than national — a tendency already well advanced in automobiles and electronics. The size difference between the large U.S.-controlled enterprise and the large European-controlled enterprise could very well decline a little. Where the asymmetry is likely to linger longest is in one of the most sensitive areas of all, the genuinely high-technology industries. Though Europe may yet find the institutional means for assembling the disconcertingly large quantities of resources that seem necessary for major advances in such fields as airframes, nuclear reactors, and so on, progress on this front is likely to be slow.

Even if the governments of the advanced countries continue to show grudging tolerance for the growth of U.S.-controlled multinational enterprises, as most of them have in recent years, it seems quite unlikely that such enterprises will increase their relative position in the world's industry and trade at the rate prevailing since the early 1950s. History may attribute part of the growth of U.S.-controlled enterprises during the past few decades, especially in the advanced countries, to two special factors: a belated introduction of the stream of innovations that U.S.-based enterprises had managed to accumulate in the war and immediate postwar period; and a temporary acceleration in Europe's demand for the products and processes in which these innovations were incorporated, generated partly by the postwar catching-up process and partly by the special stimuli associated with the creation of the European Community.

The Europeans and the Japanese can be counted on to elbow their way into some of these U.S.-dominated preserves, appropriating the designs or other elements of novelty embodied in the innovations and eroding the oligopolistic position of the U.S. leaders. The size and multinational character of U.S.-controlled enterprises, which may have been an advantage in earlier stages, will afford less advantage at the later stages. As the product is standardized and as demand grows, local enterprises in the advanced countries may be in a position to exploit all the potential economies of scale that then exist, without having to bear the costly overhead involved in maintaining an international organization of communication and control.

The production of standardized goods can be expected to continue shifting to Europe and Japan, as in the past, whether under the aegis of multinational enterprises or of local producers. What, then, are the consequences for the United States, especially if new products are not so readily forthcoming from the U.S. economy as they were during the 1940s and 1950s? There is every reason to suppose that the shift of production to Europe and Japan will slow up of its own accord. If production moved away from the United States

and if it were unable to fill the economic hole with new innovations, then the mix of products and the type of process
in the other advanced countries would begin to resemble the
American mix more closely. In this case, one major reason
for the higher labor productivity of the United States would
disappear, and labor costs in Europe and Japan — which have
provided one of the main advantages of those areas in producing standardized goods — would probably converge toward the U.S. level.

Japan is distinguished from Europe, however, in a number of respects. Until very recently, she had managed her
spectacular industrial growth without appearing to increase
her dependence on the resources of the U.S.-controlled enterprises. This stage of Japan's development could conceivably
be coming to an end. The spectacular rise of Japan's living
standards and industrial capabilities has begun to move her
toward the position of Great Britain, Germany, or France in
terms of her technological needs. Until very recently, these
needs could generally be satisfied by industrial technology
that had already been in existence for some years — hence,
by innovations that were not very closely held among foreign enterprises outside Japan. As long as the Japanese were
bidding for technology that was well known and widely dispersed in other countries, their bargaining position was relatively strong. Paradoxically, however, as nations approach
the frontier of industrial innovation, their bargaining position tends to weaken in certain respects; the technology they
are reaching for is much more closely held. Except perhaps for
the United States, there is no advanced nation in the world
capable of generating more than a fraction of the technological elements needed for a highly advanced society. As Japan
approaches that frontier, therefore, her negotiating position
in relation to U.S.-controlled enterprises could well decline.

Turning from advanced to the less developed areas, we
find that some added factors are brought into play. In the

raw materials industries, it can be foreseen that these countries will continue to press foreign-owned enterprises for a
reapportioning of the rewards and that the outcome will depend on the bargaining positions of the two parties. In industries in which the foreigner's role was most dispensable —
whether because of capital requirements, technological considerations, or questions of market access — the erosion of
the foreigner's position will be most rapid.

In the manufacturing sector, foreign-owned enterprises
may be expected to exhibit continued strength. The capacity of multinational enterprises to manage international logistical systems efficiently has been growing, stimulated by
relative declines in international transport costs and absolute
shrinkages in transport time. The growth in these enterprises has been matched by the growing needs of the less developed countries for organizational skills and export markets. The result has been that the strong underlying hostility
in those countries toward multinational enterprises engaged
in manufacturing has been held in check. True, less developed countries in the position of India, Mexico, and Brazil
— nations that have made some progress toward industrialization — have placed unremitting pressure on the more con-
spicuous multinational enterprises, compelling them to give
up lines of local activity as rapidly as national entrepreneurs
can take them over; and this sort of pressure can be expected
to continue. But there is nothing to prevent multinational
enterprises from continuing to do what they have done successfully in the past—adding new activities of increasing complexity, even as they slough off the old.

III

Political questions will also affect the future of multinational enterprises. One important set of issues has to do with
the social goals of the advanced nations. Will nations con-

tinue to emphasize such goals as the redistribution of personal income, the promotion of laggard regions, the provision of social services and the enlargement of guarantees against economic vicissitudes? The odds seem high that they will. If they do, the need of governments to feel that the main facets of the national economy are under their control will also grow. It would seem to follow that if multinational enterprises appear less controllable than national enterprises, that perception — whether justified or not — will create increasing agitation and perturbation.

Is one to assume, then, that multinational enterprises are bound to meet increasingly hostile national administrations in the advanced countries? Not inevitably. Improvements in international communication and transportation continue to generate common norms and problems among the advanced countries. Monetary and fiscal problems are more and more interrelated both within Europe and across the Atlantic; so are issues of employment and unemployment. As long as these relations grow, there is a need and a possibility of achieving accommodation.

As for the less developed countries, the main question is whether they are likely to adopt some socialist economic system that would grossly limit the role of the multinational enterprise. Just what socialism would mean for the multinational enterprise is not clear. During recent years, several genuinely socialist countries have cast about for a way of assigning a role to foreign-owned enterprises in their economies. Other less developed countries — for example, Pakistan, Tunisia and Iraq — though committed to socialism of some sort, have nevertheless cultivated a certain deliberate ambiguity over the future position to be given multinational enterprises. As India edges her way closer to socialism, it is not clear whether or not her policies toward foreign investors will grow any more restrictive.

There is one characteristic of the less developed world,

however, that it does seem safe to predict will continue —
endemic political instability. Each year during the 1960s,
something like 40 insurgencies, revolts, coups or uprisings
were reported around the world, mostly in less developed
areas. Whatever the trend of ideology may be in the less developed world, uncertainty will be the lot of the foreign
investor. Whenever one side or another in a local political
struggle seeks to rally local support, a call for firmness toward the foreign investor is sure to be a useful tactic.

IV

Most proposals for dealing with problems generated by
multinational enterprises have been special in outlook and
limited in objective.

To the extent that spokesmen for multinational enterprises see a problem, it is the unremitting governmental nip-
ping at their flanks. The U.S. government's insistence on
maintaining a system of controls over the flow of funds between U.S. parents and their overseas subsidiaries represents
one set of hurdles. The conditions imposed by other governments are another. Even after these obstacles have been
surmounted, discrimination practiced against U.S.-owned
subsidiaries established in host countries represents still another.

Contrary to the common impression, large U.S.-controlled
enterprises are remarkably reluctant to invoke the support
of the U.S. government in overcoming the obstacles created
by other governments. This seeming passivity, even when
treaty rights are being impaired, reflects the basic fact that
U.S. business interests feel most comfortable when they are
holding the U.S. government at arm's length.

There are times, of course, when governmental help is
wanted, even demanded. Managers of the larger multinational enterprises are aware, however, that trying to pit gov-

ernment against government in an effort to solve their problems could have a price in terms of ill will and retaliation. Even when the U.S. government applies pressure one cannot be sure it will work. Accordingly, when U.S.-controlled enterprises have felt foreign governments breathing down their necks, the disposition has been to find some answer that did not involve intergovernmental threat or collaboration.

Despite this general attitude, enterprises concerned with international business have been known to support intergovernmental agreements where they felt they could be held to carefully limited and selected goals. After all, the International Convention for the Protection of Industrial Property — a convention safeguarding the rights of inventors and their assignees to obtain patent protection in foreign countries — has been operating for 85 years or so. Bilateral treaties for the avoidance of double taxation have been sponsored by business interests for many years. These have been seen, however, as far less equivocal in effect and intent than any governmental initiative would be with regard to the more general problems of multinational enterprises.

Because explicit, well-defined bargains have proved useful in times past, managers of multinational enterprises have on occasion proposed that the United States might, for instance, exchange reductions in U.S. tariff schedules for guarantees that would benefit U.S.-owned subsidiary operations in foreign countries. However, such an exchange seems less than appropriate, given the character of the U.S. interests involved.

There is not much doubt that in narrowly economic terms multinational enterprises usually make a positive contribution to the countries in which they establish their subsidiaries. In terms of U.S. economic welfare, the net effect is probably positive as well, though it clearly benefits management and stockholders more than labor. In terms of the political objectives, the case is more qualified still; the tension generated by the presence of U.S.-controlled subsidiaries abroad can hardly be thought of as an unequivocal and positive contribution to U.S. foreign relations.

The question of benefits to the United States from its multinational enterprises is further complicated by uncertainty as to whether the interests should be regarded as American. Measured by equity ownership, the overseas commitments of U.S.-controlled multinational enterprises are 90 percent or more American; by sources of funds, perhaps 25 percent American; by the identity of employees, less than one percent American; and by the identity of the governments that receive their taxes, practically 100 percent foreign. Though the contribution of these enterprises to global welfare suggests that their rights and interests would still be worth fostering and protecting, it is questionable if the appropriate means for providing these safeguards is for one nation — the United States — to bargain with its tariffs to that end.

When U.S. businessmen have weighed the possibility of an intergovernmental agreement to buttress their foreign rights, they usually have preferred the promulgation of a code of fair conduct. This type of proposal assumes that businessmen will subscribe to general standards of behavior by which they will be guided in host countries. There is nothing wrong with an approach of this sort, but it is trivial in comparison with the malaise with which it deals. Commitments of this sort could not be expected to affect feelings in host countries about the effects of multinational enterprises.

If business leaders have little to propose in the way of constructive solutions, do host countries have richer suggestions? All the rhetoric to the contrary, many political leaders and members of other élite groups in host countries are well aware of the eagerness of most U.S.-controlled multinational enterprises to blend into the national environment and to adhere to the "when in Rome . . ." principle. For the local readers, the crux of the problem lies in the very nature of the multinational enterprise, namely its ability to think in terms that extend beyond a single country and to use resources located in more than one jurisdiction. These characteristics are seen as a threat by government leaders bent on full control, by local businessmen aspiring to compete, and by intellectuals hoping to overturn the status quo.

The challenge to domestic interests has caused host governments to favor schemes for sharing ownership and control in the subsidiaries of international enterprises. This sort of proposal assumes that although multinational enterprises may well perform some useful economic function when they set up their subsidiaries, the usefulness of any given subsidiary declines in the course of time. Sharing the control and requiring eventual divestiture are generally thought of as a remedy in two senses: they reduce the economic costs to the host country by cutting off the foreigner's right to perpetual rewards; and they reduce a source of political tension between the host country and the country of the parent enterprise, *e.g.*, the United States.

The trouble with a general prescription of this sort is that it makes a fundamentally wrong assumption about the actual operations of most U.S.-controlled subsidiaries abroad. As a rule, these have continually altered the scope of their activities, pushed by threats of new local competition or government pressure or stimulated by the discovery of new opportunities in the local economies. Plants that began with certain products such as radios and small motors have had to slough them off, while taking on new products such as television sets; and they have had to go from simple assembly and packaging to the manufacture of complex components and ingredients. Some subsidiaries that originally had nothing to offer in terms of market access because they were selling only in the local market have turned to exports, using the intelligence network and the distributing machinery of their affiliates in the multinational enterprise structure. In such cases a constant process of divestiture and renewal has been going on inside the organization. This provides no basis for assuming that the benefits to the host country have declined in time; the contrary could just as well be true. In narrow economic terms, a program of formal divestiture could prove hurtful rather than beneficial.

There is a difficulty of another sort with any general policy of divestiture. Multinational enterprises might not be hostile to divestiture provided it was limited to cases where the investor and the host government had foreseen and arranged for it at the time of the original investment. But this proviso would be hard to guarantee. A divestiture by a consenting enterprise could easily whet the host country's appetite for another divestiture in which the enterprise was less willing, especially if the domestic political situation made it seem useful.

Furthermore, when measured in standard economic terms, a prearranged scheme for divestiture would often be hurtful to host countries. It would tend to scare off foreign investors who had a long-term view of their investment. It would probably repel investors possessing genuinely scarce capabilities. And it would almost certainly discourage investors who were planning to use the subsidiary to produce for export to other affiliates rather than to supply the local market. Still, if host governments were prepared to accept the consequences of their policies and if divestitures were between consenting parties — that is, if they were a condition of entry laid down by the host government and accepted by the enterprise — outsiders could hardly make any objection.

The proposals discussed above are those of the obvious protagonists. What about the views of those lucky enough not to be embroiled directly in the fray? One set of neutrally proposed remedies has been based on the concept of the "world corporation" or the "U.N. corporation." Because multinational enterprises have global interests and affect many states, only a global régime, it is supposed, could provide the essential geographical symmetry. For proposals of this sort, an enterprise that expects to establish itself in many jurisdictions ought not to consist of an agglomeration of artificial persons, each created by the notarial seal of a different sovereign and each responsible to its mandates. Instead, it should be a single entity, responsible in the first instance to a world body.

While this approach may satisfy the intellectual need for symmetry between the governor and the governed, in other respects it is out of joint with the times. For it consists essentially of assuming the problem away. The underlying assumption is that nations can be persuaded to delegate the rules of corporate behavior to an international body and that the conflicts of national interest resulting from the operation of the rules will be allowed to work themselves out without direct interference by nation-states. Where the mandates imposed by the nation-states and those imposed by the higher global authority are in direct conflict, it is assumed that the mandate of the nation-state will give way to that of the global authority. One day, these assumptions may seem plausible, but not at present.

V

It is very likely that the manifest technical advantages of large enterprises and of strong governments will lead men in the future to insist on both. Adam Smith's model of a world of little firms and Karl Marx's model of a society of many benign utopian proletariats both seem grotesquely implausible. But in dealing with large concentrations of economic power, it is well to remember Lord Acton's maxim:

Power corrupts. Men with power have an extraordinary capacity to convince themselves that what they want to do coincides with what society needs done for its good. This comfortable illusion is shared as much by strong leaders of enterprise as by strong leaders of government. The challenge in social organization is to ensure that the large units on which our future societies are likely to be based act as countervailing political powers, not as mutually reinforcing ones.

The problems generated by the operations of multinational enterprises will not stand still. Despite the recrudescent nationalism of the U.S. government and those of other advanced countries during the early 1970s, the factors that have been increasing the economic and political interaction between national economies during the 1950s and 1960s are still hard at work. The flow of international communications is still increasing exponentially, stimulated by mounting efficiency and declining cost. Though international trade may be a bit inhibited by tariffs and quotas, attempts to control the international movement of ideas or capital by means of national border restrictions seem increasingly quixotic. As these elusive elements move more rapidly across international boundaries and blunt the effectiveness of national controls, a key question for the future is how long it will take for governments to find the level of tension unacceptable.

When the tension does come to be unbearable, the time for substantial action may be at hand. Then a number of steps can be envisaged.

Let us begin at the most mundane level of all, at the level of the pocketbook. As local governments are well aware, their own ability to gauge the appropriateness of the taxes that are paid by the subsidiaries of multinational enterprises is fairly limited. This fact does nothing to contribute to their sense of assurance and control. The multinational enterprises themselves also take a detailed and continuous interest in the question of local taxes. Because of the interrelated operations of their subsidiaries, the division of the profits of such enterprises among different national jurisdictions almost always unavoidably involves arbitrary allocations. As long as multinational enterprises have felt that the freedom to allocate their profits among jurisdictions offered them net advantages, they have preferred to let the problem rest in obscurity. This freedom, however, shows signs of being reduced. The curiosity of governments over how allocations are made and how they affect tax liabilities is growing speedily. Questions of international transfer pricing, overhead allocation, the use of debt in lieu of equity, and similar esoteric issues are rapidly becoming familiar concerns of many national tax officials.

A multinational approach to tax problems could take several different forms. A relatively easy response would be to enunciate some general principles applicable to all tax jurisdictions, relating, for example, to transfer pricing and the use of debt in lieu of equity, and to develop a means for settling disputes in the application of the principles. If the principles were adopted by a sufficient number of countries, they would accomplish two things: they would reduce the chances that a multinational enterprise, caught between the scissor blades of two taxing jurisdictions, would be unfairly taxed; at the same time, they would increase the assurances that such enterprises were not using their flexibility to slip between the national taxing authorities.

Still another approach would be more fundamental in character and more ambitious in reach. In view of the arbitrary nature of profits assigned to subsidiaries, it can be argued that the assessment of tax liability in any jurisdiction should be based on the proration of the consolidated profit of the multinational enterprise as a whole, according to an agreed proration formula.

A change of this sort, however, would require the United States and other countries to look on the taxable profits of their multinational enterprises in a fundamentally new light. Germany then would share in the profits generated by General Motors in the United States, while the United States would share in the profits generated by a subsidiary in Germany. The experience would be novel for both: for Germany because she has so far been entitled to look only to the German subsidiary for taxes, and for America because she has up to now confined her tax reach mainly to the parent's dividends from foreign subsidiaries.

Another problem suitable for international collaboration is the question of joint jurisdiction over subsidiaries. In essence, countries would have to be prepared by formal treaty to give up the right to reach into the jurisdiction of others in order to influence actions that they feel affect their national interests. The prospects for joint action of this sort would be greatest among countries that thought of themselves as having a common interest and a common viewpoint, and greatest with respect to those fields in which consultation appeared easiest. On these criteria, the United States would find collaborative efforts easiest with the advanced countries of Western Europe, perhaps with the European Community itself. And the fields of possible collaboration might be expected to include national policies with regard to restrictive business practices and mergers, trading-with-the-enemy policy, and the control of capital movement.

At same time, however, there would almost certainly be need for a continuous harmonization of policy wherever restraints on the exercise of sovereign power were being assumed. Substantial differences in national levels of control are tolerable, provided a channel for consultation exists. The United States, for instance, has long since resigned itself to the fact that other countries exercise more relaxed restrictions than it does over trade with the Communist world, and is prepared to permit overseas subsidiaries to impair the objectives of U.S. policies in this area. The same is also true of the antitrust field; the United States is by now ruefully aware that it must move with a certain restraint when it reaches into the jurisdictions of other countries to enforce its antitrust objectives. The formalization of procedures for consultation and the commitment to harmonization efforts, therefore, would represent no giant departure from present practices.

Undertakings of this sort might conceivably enlist some support from multinational enterprises, but they have a corollary that is likely to encounter much heavier going from that quarter: if sovereigns agree to refrain from trying to control the overseas subsidiaries of their national enterprises, the subsidiaries themselves should be treated as nationals by the host governments, and consequently should give up diplomatic support from the governments of their parent companies. These principles have cropped up repeatedly in the diplomatic history of international investment and have evoked unrestrained hostility on the part of U.S. enterprises. Known as the Calvo Clause after the Argentine minister who first advanced them, these principles have been pushed hard by Latin American governments in their efforts to cut off U.S. government support of U.S.-controlled subsidiaries. As Latin American governments generally frame the principles, they would deny all local rights and remedies to any foreign-owned subsidiary if the subsidiary called on a foreign government in a dispute with its host government.

It has to be remembered, however, that the application of governmental authority on a nondiscriminatory basis to enterprises, whether local or foreign, is far from universal; under most systems of jurisprudence, governments are free to distribute rewards and penalties to their nationals according to less obvious criteria, without running afoul of their own laws, expectations, and customs. Accordingly, a guarantee of "national treatment" in such cases does not have much content. Instead, some minimum guarantees of equitable treatment would probably have to be substituted for the standard of national treatment. Defining the concept of equitable treatment would be difficult; enforcing it would be more difficult still. Given the nature of the judicial process in many countries, it would not be feasible to leave the enforcement problem wholly to national legal systems. More likely than not, some sort of international tribunal would have to be charged with the adjudicating function.

The objective of disentangling conflicting jurisdictions, therefore, will require a series of international commitments: self-denying ordinances on the part of sovereigns to prevent their reaching into other jurisdictions and a means of international consultation to interpret them; a denial to foreign-owned subsidiaries of the right to call on the governments of their parent companies for diplomatic support; and a means of providing and enforcing commitments for the equitable treatment of the subsidiaries concerned.

The chances are that some forward motion on these agreements and procedures will be possible among the advanced nations long before similar action might be taken in the less developed world. The refusal of Latin American governments in the latter 1960s even to sign a relatively innocuous multilateral Convention on the Settlement of Investment Disputes suggests how far they are from any willingness to consider joint action in this general field. Nor does the fact that so many African countries have gone along with the agreement offer any basis for greater hope, since in many cases that was much more a recognition of weakness than an expression of collaboration; eventually, a more independent line of response is to be expected from this quarter as well.

VI

But even if most of these suggestions were adopted and enforced, many sources of tension still would remain. Foreign-owned subsidiaries and their parents would have waived rights of diplomatic support from the parent government, while the host countries would have extended guarantees of equitable treatment to the subsidiaries.

Agreements not to impose controls on outward flows of direct capital investment, let it be assumed, have been developed among the major advanced countries. Assume, too, that the division of taxes has been made a matter of joint commitment and interest among major governments. Would these measures eliminate the problems generated by multinational enterprises?

The answer is clearly no. The capability of multinational enterprises to exercise flexibility and choice would still seem oppressive in the eyes of many who had to deal with them. What more could be done? There is a certain urgency in the question, arising out of the fact that individual states are beginning to require multinational enterprises to justify major decisions in the allocation of production or of markets among facilities located in different national jurisdictions. The prospect that the various states might expand such practices, unilaterally and on an uncoordinated basis, is slightly nightmarish from the viewpoint of the multinational enterprise. In industries where such action is not uncommon, as in the oil industry, the experience of conflicting government commands already hurts at times. The international regularization of such demands would be more tolerable than the growth of unilateral actions by states.

Under what ground rules might an international organization become party to the major allocative decisions of multinational enterprises? If the broad interests of all nations are considered, a major decision of such enterprises that was otherwise consistent with the laws and policies of the nations concerned ought not to be subject to the veto of parties that felt threatened, unless the project was based on some patently "artificial" factor, suitably defined. The definition would presumably include cases such as the existence of a subsidy or of a threat coming from one of the signatory governments or of a private market-sharing agreement among enterprises.

Situations involving subsidy are an obvious problem area. Nations cannot put off much longer some joint understanding over the use of subsidies and tax concessions as incentives for the international movement of industry. The competition among advanced countries in making lavish capital grants to industry, and among less developed countries in extending broad tax exemptions to industry, should be brought under some measure of control. If all host countries were to reduce or eliminate the benefits, foreign direct investment probably would not decline very much, nor would global welfare be impaired. If less developed countries felt that they wanted to retain a limited right to extend such subsidies, however, their desires could be accommodated in the agreement. A major implication of this approach is that governments — especially the U.S. government — will be obliged to convert issues which they had once thought domestic into issues of international concern. U.S. labor, for instance, would find itself in an international forum if it sought to block the establishment of the Taiwan subsidiary of a U.S. parent.

The direction of these suggestions is clear. The basic asymmetry between multinational enterprises and national governments may be tolerable up to a point, but beyond that point there is a need to reestablish balance through accountability to a governing body multinational in scope. If this does not happen, some of the apocalyptic projections of the future of multinational enterprise will grow more plausible.

Problems and Policies Regarding Multinational Enterprises

(Reprinted from U.S. Commission for International Trade . . .
Report to The President submitted by the Commission
on International Trade and Investment Policy, 1971)

Problems and Policies Regarding Multinational Enterprises

The title of this paper requires a word or two of amplification. Problems, as is well known, are in the eye of the beholder; what is a "problem" from governments' point of view is often an advantage from the point of view of the enterprises; and what is a "problem" from the enterprises' point of view may be a solution on the part of governments.

The object of this paper is to define the problems as perceived by the various interested parties and to develop programs and policies that may be responsive. The proposals set out here are based on a number of fundamental propositions, the basis for which is to be found in my first paper, "The Economic Consequences of U.S. Foreign Direct Investment." The first of these is that the multinational enterprise has a substantial contribution to make to global welfare, if welfare is measured in economic terms. The second proposition is that many of the expressions of concern over the economic consequences of these enterprises, such as the views about their balance-of-payment effects and employment effects, are not supported by the facts. The third proposition, however, is that not all parties affected by the multinational enterprises' operations necessarily benefit equally, or indeed necessarily benefit at all; the sharing of economic

NOTE: This paper draws on materials developed for the book entitled *Sovereignty at Bay: The Multinational Spread of U.S. Enterprises* (New York: Basic Books, 1971), as part of the product of the multinational enterprise study at the Harvard Business School.

benefits between the host country and the United States and between management, capital, and labor depends on the circumstances. Finally, the clearest problems generated by the existence of the multinational enterprise are political and psychological; they stem from the fact that the multinational enterprise, as seen through the eyes of those that have to deal with it, often seems threatening in its relative flexibility and strength. The challenge is to develop policies that deal with these problems effectively while leaving room for the multinational enterprise to make its creative contribution.

I. The Host Country View

There is, of course, no single point of view on the part of host countries with respect to multinational enterprises. Some countries, such as Belgium and Thailand, seem reasonably comfortable with the presence of the foreign-owned subsidiaries of U.S. parents. Others, such as France and Japan, are much more uneasy at the possibility of a significant increase in U.S. interests. The generalizations that follow, therefore, need to be tailored to the individual case. Nonetheless, there are some generalizations that seem appropriate for host countries. And there are some differences between countries whose underlying causes seem fairly clear.

The Challenge to Elites

The subsidiaries of U.S. parent companies cannot move into an economy in significant number without affecting the relative position of various elite groups within that economy: government leaders, businessmen, and intellectuals. The impact on those groups has a good deal to do with the reactions encountered in different countries.

Consider first of all the situation in less developed countries at the early stages of their growth.[1] In those very early stages, foreign-owned subsidiaries have commonly been welcomed by the preponderance of the local leadership. The welcome was somewhat more unqualified before World War II than since. Its quality also was affected by the circumstances — often accidental and idiosyncratic in character — under which the country received its independence. Ex-colonial powers which gained their independence by struggle have tended to be chary of foreign-owned investments, while countries that acquired their independence more peacefully tended to be less resistant to foreign investment. Countries that chose "socialism," following the charisma of their first post-independence leaders, have been rather less forthcoming toward foreign investors than others; witness the case

---

[1] The observations that follow are drawn principally from W. R. Crawford, *A Century of Latin-American Thought* (Cambridge: Harvard University Press, 1961), especially pp. 116–164; A. O. Hirschman, "Ideologies of Economic Development in Latin America," in A. O. Hirschman (ed.), *Latin American Issues* (New York: Twentieth Century Fund, 1961), pp. 4–9; Leopoldo Zea, *The Latin American Mind* (trans. James H. Abbott and Lowell Dunham) (Norman, Okla.: University of Oklahoma Press, 1963), esp. pp. 77–86; Raymond Vernon, *The Dilemma of Mexico's Development* (Cambridge: Harvard University Press, 1963), pp. 39–47; Hubert Herring, *A History of Latin America* (New York: A. A. Knopf, 1955), pp. 583–625; J. F. Rippy, *Latin America* (Ann Arbor: University of Michigan Press, 1968), pp. 274–281; Jose Bello, *A History of Modern Brazil: 1889–1964* (trans. by James Taylor) (Stanford: Stanford University Press, 1966), pp. 20–76; J. F. Normano, *Brazil: A Study of Economic Types* (Chapel Hill: University of North Carolina Press, 1935), pp. 78–82; Jonathan Levin, *The Export Economies* (Cambridge: Harvard University Press, 1960), pp. 27–123; Percival Griffiths, *Modern India* (New York: Praeger, 1965), pp. 220, 282; *The Oxford History of India*, third edition (Oxford: Oxford University Press, 1958), pp. 710–713, 834–838; Matthew J. Kust, *Foreign Enterprise in India* (Chapel Hill: University of North Carolina Press, 1964), pp. 22–23; Percival Spear, *India: A Modern History* (Ann Arbor: University of Michigan Press, 1961), pp. 298–309; H. H. Smythe and M. M. Smythe, *The New Nigerian Elite* (Stanford: Stanford University Press, 1960), esp. pp. 74–92; Thomas Fillol, *Social Factors in Economic Development: The Argentine Case* (Cambridge: M.I.T. Press, 1961), pp. 40–53; and E. B. Burns, *Nationalism in Brazil* (New York: Praeger, 1968), pp. 29–127.

of Guinea and Tanzania versus that of the Ivory Coast and the Congo. At any rate, if the country concerned did extend some sort of welcome to the foreign investor in the early stages of its existence, that welcome gradually tended to become more equivocal and more qualified with the passage of time. Among the reasons for this shift was the changing position of various elite groups.

During the early stages of the development process, there were few among the local elite to whom foreign investors seemed threatening. Among government leaders, the need for help in launching the process of development generally transcended other considerations. Among local businessmen, the opportunity to become the provisioners or customers of the foreign enterprise was more important than the threat of confronting foreign competitors.

The positions of the government elite and of the industrial elite, however, changed in the course of time. Government officials gradually became unhappy as their needs for revenue exceeded the amounts being generated by the foreign-owned ventures, and as their sense of dependence seemed to grow. Local businessmen, meanwhile, came to acquire ambitions that extended beyond the role of mere provisioner and customer, to the role of partner and competitor.[2]

As for the intellectual leaders outside of government and business in the less developed countries, their disposition to welcome the appearance of foreign-owned enterprises was generally more qualified from the very first. Even when local official and local business attitudes were cordial, an undercurrent of dissent among the intellectuals often existed. The role assumed by leaders of the university and of the press in many less developed countries was the role of the outside

---

[2] See H. H. Smythe and M. M. Smythe, *The New Nigerian Elite* (Stanford: Stanford University Press, 1960) , esp. pp. 74–92; Raymond Vernon, *The Dilemma . . . op. cit.*, pp. 163–169; and Warren Deane, *The Industrialization of Sao Paulo, 1880–1945* (Austin: University of Texas Press, 1969) , pp. 135–148.

critic. From the opposition viewpoint, the appearance of the foreign investors represented a force that could well entrench the government and its supporters. The intellectuals could generally be counted on, therefore, to resist the entry of foreign investment.

Today, there is scarcely an underdeveloped country in which intellectuals have not raised a voice of strong dissent against foreign investors as a class. Significant protests have appeared in Ghana, Nigeria, India, Chile, Mexico, Brazil, Malaysia, Turkey, Pakistan, and the Philippines, among others. The reaction is not confined to the less developed world, however; it is to be found also in Canada and many countries of Europe. There are a few countries in which the prevailing mood in intellectual circles does not run strongly in this direction; but they are only a few, including Britain and Holland, for instance. Even in such friendly countries, however, there is some wistful or purposeful speculation over the possibilities of converting multinational enterprises to structures that are more local in character without losing the benefits of multinationality.

The Challenge to Ideologies

It is not easy to draw the line between a threat to personal position and a threat to a deeply held ideology. Some of the resistance of elites in host countries, especially those in underdeveloped economies, may well be more ideological than personal.

The ideological basis on which foreign-owned investment is resisted goes back a long way. Some of it is Marxist-Leninist in its underpinnings. Much more, however, is nationalistic in nature, even when it uses the language and concepts of Marxist ideology.

The ideological assertions regarding the impact of multinational enterprises tend to change over time, in order to keep abreast of changes in the multinational enterprises themselves. In Latin America, for instance, it was generally assumed until the mid-1950s that foreign investors were interested solely in the exploitation of raw materials and could not be persuaded to invest extensively in manufacturing facilities. Because of that assumption, it was easy to link the drawbacks of foreign investment to the drawbacks of raw material exporting. These links were provided by the well-known propositions of the Economic Commission for Latin America and of Raul Prebisch, according to which countries that specialized in exporting raw materials suffered from deteriorating terms of trade, immiscible growth, and so on.

When it became evident in the late 1950s that foreign-owned investment was going extensively into the manufacturing industries, the ideological rationalizations shifted. The argument against the foreign-owned investment then began to take the form of a protest against the exploitation or the low-wage situation of the country. Subsequently, when it became clear that as a rule foreign-owned investors paid more than prevailing local wages, the argument was developed that these excess payments were being used to buy out the industrial working class and to abort their proper role as members of a revolutionary proletariat. In addition, there was growing protest that the local partners in joint ventures were becoming indigenous Robber Barons in their respective economies.

The assumption in most quarters during the late 1950s also had been that foreign-owned manufacturing subsidiaries could only be persuaded to engage in import-substitution for the local market, and could not be persuaded to export. Today, as it is beginning to grow clear that foreign-owned subsidiaries are exporting manufactured products in some volume, the argument is shifting once again. It is pointed out that the exported products, being standardized and price-sensitive as a rule, have many of the economic characteristics of raw materials and hence are poor media for improving the long-run export position of the less developed countries.

There are various lessons to be drawn from this recital. One of them is that the tension generated by foreign-owned subsidiaries is to some extent independent of what the subsidiary does; that the overt rationalizations for the existence of the tension will shift as the function of the subsidiary shifts. One must probe beneath the overt rationalizations, therefore, to find more deep-seated causes of the tension.

The Clash of Cultures

Part of the tension, it may well be, has deep-seated cultural roots. That possibility is better illustrated in the case of a number of advanced countries, where extensive studies of the cultural background offer rich materials on which to test this general proposition. Let me illuminate the point by reviewing briefly some of the differences in business-government relations between the United States, the United Kingdom, France, and Japan.[3]

In the case of the United States, there have been a number of persistent threads in the long history of business-government relations which distinguish this country from most other advanced economies.

The first of these is the relatively high social status of businessmen in U.S. society; as the Horatio Alger novels attest, the theme of the successful businessman has been as a folk-hero exceedingly strong in U.S. culture for a very long time. On the other hand, in classic Hegelian contradiction, there

---

[3] The literature on the subject is extensive. For illustrative sources see Noel Branton, *The Economic Organization of Modern Britain* (London: English Universities Press, 1966) ; Andrew Shonfield, *Modern Capitalism* (London: Oxford University Press, 1965) ; J. H. McArthur and B. R. Scott, *Industrial Planning in France* (Boston: Division of Research, Harvard Business School, 1969) ; Stephen Cohen, *Modern Capitalist Planning: The French Model* (Cambridge: Harvard University Press, 1969) ; M. Y. Yoshino, *Japan's Managerial System: Tradition and Innovation* (Cambridge: M.I.T. Press, 1968) ; and Ryusaku Tsunoda, W. T. de Bary, and Donald Keene (eds.) , *Sources of the Japanese Tradition* (New York: Columbia University Press, 1958) .

has been a deep-seated mistrust in the United States toward the concentration of economic power that big business was thought to represent. This mistrust has manifested itself in numerous ways in U.S. political history, from the passage of the Sherman Act and the Clayton Act on the one hand to the promulgation of the Public Utility Holding Company Act on the other.

Against this background, the general U.S. approach toward the regulation of business transactions has been either to leave them alone or to prohibit them. Although some areas of business activity have been subjected to detailed regulations, the regulatory approach is a good deal less important in the United States than it is elsewhere. Where regulation does exist, the regulatory style of U.S. government agencies, is mechanistic, nondiscriminatory, and arm's length, as compared with the style of other countries. All of these elements are important, but the arm's-length quality is especially so.

It would be reckless to attempt to explain the arm's-length quality of U.S. administration in cultural terms. For present purposes, it is only necessary to point out that U.S. businessmen confront a governmental apparatus that is extraordinarily fractionated and diffused, as compared with most other modern states. All three branches of the U.S. government have some power to legislate, adjudicate, and execute. That fact, coupled with the distribution of relevant powers between the states and the federal government, makes it exceedingly difficult for the public and the private sector to collaborate on a very broad basis. There are some rather obvious exceptions, of course: the regulated industries such as the airlines; the major defense contractors, such as the airframe producers; and to a more limited extent, the major oil companies. By comparison with other countries, however, these exceptions do not cover a very wide area.

There is a widespread notion, both at home and abroad, that a close collaboration exists between U.S. industry on the one hand and U.S. government on the other, forming collectively an expensive force bent on gaining control of the world economy. That impression is grossly at variance with the actual facts. But from time to time the policies of the United States have lent support to this widespread perception: by the landing of the Marines in distant countries once or twice every decade; by the passage of legislation such as the Hickenlooper Amendment; and by various other measures that would be consistent with the collaboration theory. Even a small amount of collaborative behavior between business and government can be frightening to other nations, if the collaboration is undertaken by such great powers as the U.S. government and U.S. business overseas.

Business-government relations in the United Kingdom display some obvious similarities to those in the United States. The capacity of the United Kingdom to tolerate U.S.-controlled investments without much tension may stem in part from those similarities. True, there are marked differences in such relations as well; but these differences are small as compared with most other countries.

The British, for instance, share some of the U.S. distaste for privilege and monopoly on the part of business. True, their responses to problems of this sort have been later, milder, and more equivocal than those of the United States. When eventually they began to appear in a series of enactments beginning with the Restrictive Practices Acts of 1948, they reflected a much less doctrinaire view of the nature of "undesirable" restraints of trade and "undesirable" monopolies. But they represented a view that was shared on both sides of the Atlantic.

In one fundamental respect, the British environment and the U.S. environment are nearly identical. In both cases, there is a basic presumption shared by both business and government that governmental regulatory powers will normally be applied on a nondiscriminatory basis — that discrimination, preference, and the chosen instrument approach represent the exceptional case, not the preferred state. This approach sits well with the arm's-length habits and expectations of U.S. business.

One difference of some significance between the British approach and the U.S. approach to business-government relations is the greater reliance of the British on voluntary schemes of business regulation. The British are conditioned to the view that any class of enterprise which for a long time has exercised some kind of prerogative in the economy, whatever the basis for that prerogative, presumptively ought to be allowed to continue to practice its acquired rights. On the other hand, there is a constraining proposition which accompanies this approach: the view that anybody that has such rights should not abuse them. As a result, "voluntary" controls schemes are much more common, more feasible, and more effective in the British environment than in the United States.

The differences between U.S. practice and U.K. norms are especially marked in one field — in that of external relations. Here the long British tradition, under which the flag has tended to follow trade, still seems to have some vestigial influence. In any event, the degree of collaboration between British business and British government outside of Britain is very much closer than that in the case of the United States.

Moving from the British case to the French case, the similarities with the United States decrease while the differences grow large. In this instance, the U.S. businessman encounters a set of relationships that are almost wholly foreign to his experience.

In France, both the concept of arm's-length relationship and the notion of nondiscrimination in the exercise of governmental power evaporate. To be sure, businessmen have rights; but they are rights that depend upon an explicit and formal grant from the state, not upon any general presumption in favor of noninterference or nondiscrimination. Moreover, until recently, innovation and change were not regarded as a virtue when initiated by businessmen. Quite the contrary. The emphasis was on harmony and stability, rather than on growth and profit. A great deal of that sentiment still remains, as part of the background of relations between French business and French government. When initiatives were forthcoming from the government in order to induce change, as has commonly been the case, resort to the use of chosen instruments has been perfectly easy and natural, violating no deeply held convictions to the contrary on the part of the French public.

In the range of country cases considered here, Japan sits at the far extreme from the United States. Reams have been written about the outstanding characteristics of contemporary Japanese culture. That culture incorporates some concepts that have proved extraordinarily useful in an industrial society, including a widespread commitment to goal attainment and a concept of shared responsibility within any group assigned to achieve a given goal. The limits of "the group," however, are much more readily visible to the Japanese eye than to that of the outsider. Sometimes the group is a family; sometimes an industry; and sometimes — especially in matters that relate to negotiations with foreigners — the whole of the Japanese economy.

The line that is drawn between the public and the private sector in Japan is not nearly so clear as in many other Western countries. From the very first, economic tasks assigned to the two sectors have been determined pragmatically, rather than on the basis of some deep-seated ideology. Business leaders have readily become ministers in government; and ministers have easily returned to business. This process has not been accompanied by any of the soul-searching and the conflict-of-interest questions that arise when similar events occur in the United States.

Today, as is well known, the policies of Japanese business and Japanese government are coordinated largely through two institutions: the banking system and the Ministry of

onal Trade and Industry (MITI). For external
, MITI puts up a common front, on the basis of
that are worked out with Japanese industry. Once
that iront is created, it is exceedingly difficult for any foreigner to negotiate independently with any Japanese entity.

There are a number of generalizations to be drawn from
these brief observations. The capacity of each of these cul-
tures to tolerate outsiders runs in the order in which they
are presented: from the United States to the U.K. to France
to Japan. The Japanese find it particularly difficult to tolerate the existence within the Japanese society of someone
who is not a part of "the group." The extent to which governments are selective in their treatment of business firms
runs in roughly the same order. The United States is least
capable of being selective in its handling of business, while
the Japanese are probably most capable in engaging in such
selectivity. There is a similar ranking in the degree to
which nationals are monitored by their respective governments when such nationals engage in major activities outside the boundaries of their country. In this case, again, the
United States is at the low end of the monitoring activity,
while Japan is at the high end of such activity.

In sum, the tension generated by the presence of U.S. enterprises seems highest where the differences between the
norms of the local culture and the U.S. are greatest. As long
as those differences persist, as they surely will, tension may
be the normal state of being.

II. Control and Jurisdiction

So far the emphasis has been on the special issues that generate tension in the host countries. But the tension that fol-
lows in the trail of multinational enterprise operations is
not limited to host countries. It also appears from time to

time in the United States. What are these more general sources of difficulty?

Loss of Control

The multinational enterprise is perceived by those that deal with it as an entity with an extraordinary capacity for flexibility and choice. It is thought capable of choosing between different locations for the establishment production and research facilities, for the allocation of markets, for the storing of its surplus funds, and so on. Stated another way, the multinational enterprise is thought of as mobile between national economies, while those with whom it bargains — including government and labor — are fixed to a particular piece of national real estate. The perception of mobility is probably exaggerated by those that do not share it; but there is not much doubt that such mobility does exist. Indeed, this element of choice is one of the major strengths of the multinational enterprise as a contributor to global welfare.

Nevertheless, this aspect of the operations of multinational enterprise adds to the unease not only of interests in the host countries but also of interests in the United States. Take some of the reactions of U.S. labor to the multinational enterprise. Labor economists are presumably well aware that the effect of freezing U.S. jobs in existing job patterns would eventually reduce U.S. incomes, pushing them toward the levels existing in other countries; that the essence of any U.S. strategy for maintaining the world's highest per capita income is to shift constantly out of the lines in which others can compete into those in which they cannot. It is one thing to accept that ineluctable proposition in the abstract; it is another, however, to confront the business decision maker across the bargaining table who seems to be charged with deciding when the shift will take place. Irrespective of the inevitability — even the desirability — of the shift in the long run, the short-run negotiating advantage that the representative of the mul-

tinational enterprise may appear to have is exceedingly difficult for any negotiator to endure.

The sense of uneasiness over the seeming options of multinational enterprise is not confined to American labor, however. It is also to be found in the reactions of other governments, with a degree of intensity that depends upon the
capacity of the government to tolerate uncertainty. Accordingly, the Japanese and the French — who put heavy emphasis
upon control and predictability in the economy — find the
presence of the multinational enterprise less tolerable than,
say, the British and the Dutch. There are some signs that the
U.S. government itself occasionally feels uneasy over the
operations of multinational enterprise, sensing the limits on
its own control over their operations. These indications of
uneasiness appear from time to time in the usual fields: antitrust, trading with the enemy, and capital movements.

The capacity of the multinational enterprise to choose
among alternative locations generates a particularly acute
form of uneasiness in connection with the rivalries of member countries that form part of a Common Market area. In the
European Economic Community, for instance, the French
have been particularly disturbed over the operations of multinational enterprises because of their fear that such enterprises, if discouraged from establishing themselves in France,
would simply set up business in Belgium or Italy. In a similar vein, the Mexicans have been greatly concerned over
the possibility that multinational enterprises might penetrate
the Latin American Free Trade Area by subsidiaries established in, say, Colombia. The same kind of strain is visible
from time to time in the Central American Common Market.

This special concern is a realistic reflection of the fact
that multinational enterprises take the potential opportunities of free trade areas a good deal more seriously than do the
national firms of the constituent countries. The reasons are
evident: a U.S. firm that is setting up a subsidiary in the
European Community has less reason for rejecting a loca-

tion in, say, Sardinia than would a French firm that is already nicely settled in Lille or Nancy. By the same token, U.S.-owned enterprises that are setting up subsidiaries in foreign countries are much more responsive to local programs that offer subsidies for settling in backward areas of the country. As a result, governments find themselves paying embarrassingly high proportions of their subsidy funds to foreign-owned subsidiaries.[4]

The Problem of Jurisdictional Conflict

Every international transaction has two sides and, having two sides, is subject to the reach of two different sovereigns. A state is unlikely to surrender control over its end of an international transaction unless it is also prepared to accept the consequences that go with relinquishing control over the transaction.

The result is that governments are frequently involved in conflicts with regard to international transactions — transactions that one sovereign may want to promote and the other sovereign want to prevent. When the United States is one of those sovereigns, the measure of nervousness and resentment exhibited by the other side is greater than usual, given the relative size and strength of the U.S. economy. This issue, of course, is not one that is unique to the multinational enterprise. Its relation to the multinational enterprise is generated by the fact that such entities account for so high a proportion of international transactions.

---

[4] About half of the large U.S. enterprises with subsidiaries in Latin America claim to be engaged in integrated planning that assumes the existence of the Latin American Free Trade Area. *Business International*, "Report to the Interamerican Development Bank: Study of Multinational Companies" (New York, 1968), mimeo., p. 37. The report provides numerous illustrations of intra-regional sourcing. Though no similar data exist for indigenously owned Latin American firms, there is not much doubt that their perspective is far more limited. Jose de la Torre, "Exports of Manufactured Goods from Developing Countries: Marketing Factors and the Role of Foreign Enterprise" (unpublished D.B.A. thesis, Harvard Business School, 1971), Chap. 6, p. 35.

There is another problem of overlapping jurisdictions, however, in which the multinational enterprise plays a very special role. From time to time, the U.S. government tries to influence the behavior not merely of the U.S. parent but also of other entities in the multinational enterprise structure, including overseas subsidiaries. In essence, that is what the United States was trying to do when it imposed capital export controls on overseas investments. In this case, the instructions issued to the parent were instructions that were intended to govern the behavior of the overseas subsidiary in such matters as the declaration of dividends, the remission of cash, the generation of imports, and so on. Much the same could be said with respect to the trading-with-the-enemy policies of the U.S. government; in these cases, the object was to oblige overseas subsidiaries to refrain from undertaking transactions with the enemy even when these transactions were perfectly acceptable to the government. Another well-known illustration of the same problem has had to do with the antitrust laws. The U.S. government has found itself constantly reaching into the jurisdictions of other countries in order to influence the behavior of U.S.-controlled subsidiaries in those countries.

The antitrust laws have proved particularly irritating because at times the reach of the United States government has gone even further, seeking to affect the alleged foreign co-conspirators of U.S. firms, whatever the ownership of the co-conspirators might be. Although this effort at the extension of national jurisdiction is not in violation of accepted principles of international law,[5] its application by the United States was deeply resented by other countries. This resentment was especially great on the part of those countries that looked at private agreements as desirable in the interests of

---

[5] *United States v. Aluminum Co. of America*, 148 F. 2d 416, 443 (2d Cir. 1945). For an authoritative discussion of the extraterritoriality issue in U.S. antitrust law, see W. L. Fulgate, "The International Aspects of the United

stabilizing or rationalizing industrial activities within their borders.

Summing Up

The list of governmental concerns that have been elaborated in the last few pages could no doubt be matched by an equally persuasive list enumerating the advantages of multinational enterprises and the advantages of the consequences flowing from their existence. Although the presence of the U.S.-controlled subsidiary may represent a challenge to some of the elite groups in the host country, it also generates support for other elite groups; although the activities of the multinational enterprise may clash with some ideologies, it lends support to others; although it may be inconsistent with some strains of European culture, it may be helpful to others; although it may create impediments for rationalization policies in some European countries, it contributes to a more vigorous competition in other countries and other sectors. In a world that weighed benefits against costs on some objectively calibrated basis, it may be that governments would tend to take a more relaxed view toward U.S.-controlled enterprises. But reality is something else again. The presence of a large, imperfectly controlled foreign element, associated with considerable strength and flexibility, constitutes a source of psychic pain that is so strong in some countries as to overwhelm and cancel out any perceived benefits.

III. Government Measures

The measures that governments take in response to their perceived problems are the source of many of the grievances of multinational enterprises. Some governmental measures,

---

States Antitrust Laws," presented at the International Conference on Monopolies, Mergers and Restrictive Practices (London, Sept. 1969), mimeo.

of course, generate a larger sense of grievance than others. Practically all of them, insofar as they represent a narrowing of choice or a competitive burden for the foreign investor, constitute a source of grievance on his part.

One response of governments consists of excluding foreign-owned enterprises from certain areas of activity. Practically all countries, including the United States, sharply limit the right of foreign-owned subsidiaries to participate in industries such as ordnance and aircraft, public broadcasting, coastal shipping, banking, and minerals exploitation on public lands. France and Japan, among others, go much further. In the case of France, foreign-owned oil companies have been limited in their activities for nearly 50 years; and all foreign-owned enterprises have been systematically screened for the past 10 years. In Japan throughout its national life, drastic limitations were placed on foreign rights of entry; the recent trend toward liberalization in this regard has been undertaken with the utmost reluctance and has involved a series of very false starts. Even Britain and Germany, though associated with a relaxed attitude toward foreign-owned enterprises, have been exhibiting occasional misgivings over the intrusion of such enterprises in "sensitive" industries. That sensitivity occasionally manifests itself in the United States as well.[6]

Apart from prohibiting foreign investment in specified areas of activity, governments have commonly laid down conditions governing foreign investment in other areas. One common condition has been that the foreigners should take on local partners in joint ventures. The motivations for

---

[6] Indeed, a leading U.S. Congressman has expressed concern that, in view of the British government's large minority stock ownership in British Petroleum, the company's acquisition of Sohio in the United States could create a Trojan horse in the U.S. economy. "Europeans Irked by U.S. Trust Role," *New York Times*, Oct. 13, 1969, p. 71.

that condition have been mixed. In part, it has been assumed that joint ventures would function in the interests of the local economy more surely than wholly-owned subsidiaries; but, in part, the motivation has been to benefit members of the local industrial community by helping them acquire equity at bargain rates. The other requirements that have been placed on foreign-owned subsidiaries have included commitments to avoid the use of local credit, commitments to produce certain stated quantities of product, commitments to export a certain proportion of goods, commitments to train local labor up to management positions, and so on.

Official requirements that lay special conditions on foreign-owned subsidiaries are rapidly increasing in scope and character. As advanced nations have begun to develop explicit policies for the development of new industries, they have begun to dispense grants and subsidies in support of those policies. For example, subsidies have been dispensed in support of industrial research. In that case, understandably, governments as a rule have not been anxious to subsidize the research of U.S.-owned subsidiaries; accordingly, they have been careful to channel their funds to national enterprises that were locally owned. The same general policy has been followed with respect to the extension of credits for modernization and improvement of plants. It is quite clear, for instance, that the Industrial Reorganization Corporation in Great Britain and the Institut de Developpement Industriel in France would be loath to direct their assistance to enterprises that were not indigenously owned.

More generally, the disposition of public agencies to favor locally owned producers is being formalized and strengthened in many countries. This is especially evident, for instance, with regard to procurement policies, especially when the procurement involves advanced products. The United Kingdom and France discriminate overtly in the procurement of products such as computers [7] and nuclear plants, while Japan goes a great deal further and excludes foreigners from supplying practically anything to government agencies.[8] This policy is not to be confused with the U.S. "Buy American" policy, a policy which is directed at imports of foreign goods, not at those produced on U.S. soil. In the European and Japanese cases, that preference is extended to exclude domestic goods, if such domestic goods were produced in foreign-owned plants.

The disposition on the part of governments to distinguish between national corporations that are foreign owned and those that are locally owned goes even further in some cases. In the United Kingdom, it influences the views of the Monopolies Commission regarding the tolerability of monopolies in the local market. If the monopolies are local in ownership the tolerance of their existence is greater than if they are foreign owned.

Many of the countries that engage in practices of the sort just described have undertaken treaty commitments to grant national treatment to U.S.-owned enterprises in their jurisdictions. Some of these practices no doubt are inconsistent with such treaty obligations. But the pressures that are pushing governments in the direction of distinguishing foreign-owned corporations from those locally owned are too strong to be resisted on such grounds.

There is one more line of governmental action that generates a sense of grievance among multinational enterprises. This is the situation in which two governments, each eager to bend the activities of the multinational enterprise to serve its needs, issue direct conflicting demands to the management of the enterprise. A classic case was one in which the head-

---

[7] See, for instance, "Computers: Buy British, Sell American," *The Economist*, March 7, 1970, p. 63.

[8] Leon Hollerman, *Japan's Dependence on the World Economy* (Princeton: Princeton University Press, 1967) , p. 260.

quarters of a multinational enterprise received a communication from the U.S. Department of Commerce and one from the U.K. Board of Trade urging it simultaneously to increase its exports in both directions across the Atlantic.

But there are more serious cases of a similar sort. One has to do with conflicts among the states as to what constitutes taxable income. In some instances, these conflicts can generate levies upon a given source of income that are close to confiscatory levels.

Another instance, already suggested, involves action in the field of antitrust. There is no serious difficulty with cases in which U.S.-owned subsidiaries abroad are explicitly being directed by foreign governments to engage in some kind of restrictive action. The difficult cases are those in which the U.S. management knows that undertaking measures that would be pleasing to the host government runs the risk of generating an antitrust suit in the United States; or, conversely, that conforming to the pressures of the U.S. Antitrust Division would be displeasing to their overseas host governments. Finally, there is the case of capital export controls. Although I am not yet aware of any such case, I confidently anticipate the day when, by formal action, a foreign government will prohibit one of the U.S.-owned subsidiaries in its jurisdiction from conforming to the requirements of the U.S. government controls.

In sum, the concept that corporations acquired by foreigners stand in a different position under local law from corporations that are indigenously owned is gaining greatly in strength in many countries of the world. That concept is not altogether new, but the scope and variety of applications of the distinction are going very fast. If there is any element in the international situation that may yet lead the management of U.S.-controlled multinational enterprises to search for a new modus operandi, it will be the continued growth of this tendency.

IV. Responses to the Problems

The Question of Timing

All the main factors that have generated the "problems" associated with multinational enterprises promise to grow over the years. As transportation and communication improve in quality and decline in cost, enterprises will continue to expand their horizons; business opportunities and business threats will be more readily visible from long distances and will lead to quicker and more frequent international responses. Meanwhile, nation-states are likely to find themselves increasingly frustrated by the growing entanglements between their national economies and those of other countries, and by the limitations on their ability to control the forces that determine their economic and political future. Over the long run, therefore, the disposition to search for some new basis to regularize the activities of multinational enterprises promises to grow.

Over the shorter run, the proposals appear somewhat different. For the present, the less developed countries are much too suspicious of the intentions and motives of the United States to engage in any joint efforts at regularizing the position of the multinational enterprises, except perhaps in terms of regional schemes for their control. And Europe is so preoccupied with broadening and developing the structure of the European Communities that it may seem for the present to have little time for much else.

The history of U.S. negotiations with the European Communities, however, suggests that their very process of internal negotiation will improve the conditions for external negotiation; that the problems they encounter in their internal deliberations will at times suggest the desirability of negotiation on their external relations. This could well be the case with regard to company law, taxation, and capital movements during the next few years. The question is whether the U.S. itself will then be in a position to know its own mind, to sense the opportunity for action, and to frame the necessary initiatives.

U.S. Capital Export Controls

One preliminary step, by way of clearing the decks, would be to get rid of the present U.S. controls over foreign direct investment. I assume that there is a presumption against restrictive measures of this sort unless the measures are responsive to some explicit national need. In this case, as my first paper indicated, the evidence fails to indicate that any U.S. purpose is being served by the measures — neither balance-of-payment objectives nor employment objectives nor any other. As long as the measures are in force, they simply serve to remind other countries of the capacity and disposition of the United States to take unilateral action even if it affects multinational interests.

Ordinary prudence suggests that the dismantling of the controls should be done as a phased withdrawal, not as a single act. But the time involved in withdrawing from the program need not exceed a period on the order of eighteen months or two years. In a succeeding section, I shall be going a step further and shall be proposing that the United States sponsor an international agreement among advanced countries to prevent the unilateral application of export controls over direct investment; but that kind of initiative can only be launched in a wider context.

Negotiating for U.S. Capital Entry

There seems no compelling reason to retain the present U.S. restraints on the freedom of U.S. enterprises to enlarge their overseas operations. Whether and how the United States should negotiate with other countries to widen U.S. investment opportunities abroad, however, is another question.

Among the proposed approaches of this sort that seems highly questionable on its merits is a proposal that the U.S. should negotiate, à la GATT, for the entry of specified U.S. industries into specified countries — automobiles into Japan, for instance; or indeed, that U.S. tariff concessions might even be swapped for such entry rights.

The proposal bristles with difficulties. If there were more time and space, perhaps all these difficulties could be adequately explored. At the very outset, however, there is the question that cannot be avoided: What is the nature of the U.S. interest being served by such a bargain?

Remember that U.S.-owned subsidiaries overseas are an odd amalgam of things: an equity interest that is predominantly American; a management interest that is part American, part local; an interest in tax revenues that is partly American but mostly local; an interest in the debt of the enterprise that is mostly non-American; and a labor interest that is overwhelmingly non-American. When Ford or General Motors set up a subsidiary in Japan, therefore, the action contributes to all sorts of interests: partly U.S., partly Japanese, largely global. For the United States to bargain U.S. tariff rates in order to increase the right of investors to make this sort of contribution has a curiously lopsided ring. Apart from the many technical questions that this approach raises, it seems a nonstarter simply in terms of the basic balance of interests involved.

Reducing Tension: The Fair-Conduct Code

If the multinational enterprise is to have a chance to express its creative potentials fully in a global society, the tensions that are generated by its presence will have to be contained. There are numerous ways for trying to achieve that objective.

If there is any view common to the U.S.-controlled multinational enterprises regarding the appropriate line of response, it is the view that sensible businessmen can be relied upon to avoid business behavior that might prove itself destructive in the long run. Governmental action may be necessary to deal with a few special problems, according to this view; but agreements such as the long-standing International Convention for the Protection of Industrial Property or bilateral treaties to avoid double taxation are quite enough, according to this view, to deal with the intergovernmental aspects of the problem.

When spokesmen for U.S. business have deviated from this general line, they have sometimes proposed that multinational enterprises might agree to adhere to a "code of fair conduct," including a commitment to adhere carefully to the provisions of local law, to respect local custom, to train local workers for responsible jobs, to support local social projects, and so on. The attraction of accepting such a code, from the viewpoint of many businessmen, stems from the fact that it fairly well describes their present behavior and requires few changes in practice or outlook. As a response to the tensions that have been described earlier, however, it is inadequate. Its inadequacy, of course, stems from the fact that it fails to see the problem as others see it.

Reducing Tension: The Divestiture Issue

Another approach, commonly espoused by host governments in less developed countries and by some sources in the advanced countries, contemplates the eventual divestiture by multinational enterprises of their interests in local subsidiaries. The general assumption behind their proposals is that multinational enterprises perform a useful function at the time at which they set up any of their subsidiaries, but that the function declines over time. On this assumption, the object is to ensure that the multinational enterprise separates itself from the subsidiary at the time at which its net contribution to the host country begins to disappear.[9]

The facts regarding the operations of multinational enterprises abroad are not inconsistent with the assumption that benefits may decline over time. The trouble, of course, is that a conclusion of this sort is much too simple. As long as multinational enterprises continue to broaden, deepen, and complicate their role in the subsidiaries that they establish in those countries, their contribution to those economies may be unending. A program of divestiture that cuts off this process could be hurtful to the governments that were demanding it.

Another fundamental problem that reduces the practicability of a divestiture program is the great gap that often exists between the value of a subsidiary as part of a multinational enterprise system and the value of that same entity when separated from the system. An automobile assembly plant that is part of a multinational system may be of great value as long as it is attached to the system, but of little value once it is separated. This means that any effort to establish an appropriate price in connection with the divestiture will lead to major difficulties.

Still another question is whether any significant number of enterprises could be expected to set up their subsidiaries if they faced the possibility of eventual divestiture. It seems plausible to assume that in circumstances of this sort the foreign investors who went ahead would be those with the

---

[9] A. O. Hirschman, *How to Divest in Latin America and Why?* (Princeton: Princeton University Press, 1969), Essays in *International Finance*, no. 76; P. N. Rosenstein-Rodan, *Multinational Investment in the Framework of Latin American Integration*, Report presented at the Round Table of the Board of Governors (Bogota, Colombia: Inter-American Development Bank, April 1968), pp. 66–78. For a more qualified endorsement of the approach, see C. F. Carlos Diaz Alejandro, *Direct Foreign Investment in Latin America*, Center Paper no. 150, Yale University, Economic Growth Center, 1970, pp. 334–336.

strongest penchant for quick profits and those with the weakest desire to enlarge the functions of the subsidiary.

But these are problems that are more appropriately the concern of the host country than of the multinational enterprise. It is for host countries to reckon whether the relaxation of tension associated with the prospect of ultimate divestiture is worth the economic cost that such a choice may entail. Even if the arrangements are hurtful in economic terms, the fact that they are between consenting adults has a bearing. And if they reduce political tensions, the economic harm they do may well be worth the cost.

As a practical matter, an investor who was prepared to contemplate an ultimate divestiture at the outset of his operation would probably demand undisturbed possession of the subsidiary on the order of twelve or fifteen years. Moreover, the arrangement, instead of contemplating inevitable sale, could better be in the form of an option on the part of local interests to buy at the end of the period; this would provide some protection against the possibility that, by the time the end of the period was in sight, the local government might prefer to extend the option rather than to exercise it, given the alternative uses it would have for investment fund at that time and given the nature of the foreigners' operations. AID might even give some thought to how it could use its extended-risk insurance program in order to guarantee prospective investors against the risk that the host government might fail to perform in accordance with the provisions of the agreed option, or against the risk that the investor might not receive some minimum upset price under the terms of the option.

Reducing Tension: The Tax Issue

One subject that contributes to the levels of tension associated with the activities of multinational enterprises is the question of taxes. Until recently, such enterprises were fairly free to allocate their costs, adjust their transfer prices, and arrange their affairs, in order to minimize the aggregate burden of national taxes. That freedom is gradually being curtailed. Government authorities are becoming· slightly more sophisticated and more aggressive in tax matters. The use of tax safe-haven companies is being somewhat curtailed. The tendency toward a greater tax pinch is growing, a fact that should predispose multinational enterprises to consider seriously whether they are prepared to accept a different kind of international regime in the tax field.

Heretofore, cooperative governmental action in this area has been confined to bilateral tax treaties. It could well be, however, that this approach will prove inadequate. In any event, inadequate or not, the approach could well be replaced by another that might contribute to a decline in the level of tensions.

One such approach is the development of a set of multinational principles applicable to all tax jurisdictions, governing the calculation of profit for tax purposes. Such principles could cover problems in the field of transfer pricing, problems involving the use of debt in lieu of equity, and problems relating to the allocation of costs. These rules, like the rules of bilateral tax treaties, could conceivably reduce the possibility that multinational enterprises might be caught between the scissor blades of two taxing jurisdictions. At the same time, however, it would increase the assurances to governments that such enterprises were not slipping between the national tax jurisdictions.

There is a more fundamental and more ambitious approach that might be considered. This is an approach based on the principle that the operations of the individual subsidiaries of multinational enterprises are inescapably interrelated and that the assignment of the profits to each of them unavoidably involves large elements of the arbitrary. The assessment of tax liability in any jurisdiction, therefore, ought to be based upon a prorationing of the consolidated profit of the multinational enterprise as a whole.

It will be recognized at once that this is the principle generally followed by the several states of the United States. The analogy to the U.S. interstate system, however, indicates how profound the proposed change would be. Such a change, for instance, would require the United States and other countries to look upon profits generated abroad in a wholly new light. These profits would be taxable to all jurisdictions as earned. At the same time, the rules for the calculation of profit would have to be harmonized in some measure, local deviations being kept within bounds. The odds are that this approach could only be followed in the first instance by the advanced countries collectively; it would be some time before many of the less developed countries would see it in their interests to proceed on these lines.

Reducing Tensions: The Sorting Out of Jurisdictions

Perhaps the most flamboyant source of the tension that goes with the operations of multinational enterprises is the occasional overlap and clash of national jurisdictions. The tax issue is a familiar manifestation of that problem, but there are more difficult and more sensitive areas in which the problem appears. If real progress is to be made on this issue, several different kinds of agreement would have to be achieved simultaneously.

In the first place, countries engaged in any collaborative effort in this area would have to begin by accepting a set of self-denying ordinances. They would have to be prepared to give up the precious right to reach into the jurisdictions of others in order to influence actions affecting their national interests. The areas in which they gave up such rights would probably have to be explicitly specified. The obvious candidates include the field of restrictive business practices and mergers, trading-with-the-enemy regulations, and the control of capital movements. On subjects such as these, governments would undertake not to try to shape the behavior of the overseas subsidiaries of their national companies by means of direct injunction or by coercion of the parent.

Commitments of that sort would not be forthcoming, however, unless at the same time there were also provisions for some continuous efforts at the harmonization of national policy in these fields. Such efforts need not lead to identical national policy. The United States has long since learned that it can live comfortably alongside friendly countries even if they refuse to pursue precisely the same policies in these sensitive fields. But countries would be loath to give up their rights to reach outward if they thought that there were no possible means by which very large differences in national policy could be somewhat narrowed. Accordingly, the self-denying ordinances would probably have to be accompanied by a mechanism for the harmonization of policies among the nations concerned.

If overseas subsidiaries are to lie beyond the reach of the governments of their parent companies, the corollary principle is that they should be looked upon unambiguously as the nationals of their host governments. That corollary, which underlies the well-known Calvo Clause in American diplomatic history, has always been bitterly resisted by the United States. In essence, the Calvo Clause provides that the local subsidiaries of foreign-owned enterprises will be treated on the same basis as any other national in the host country, and that such subsidiaries will lose any rights of access to the diplomatic support of foreign governments.

One of the difficulties of the approach, of course, is that "national treatment" in most jurisdictions of the world carries no connotation of nondiscriminatory treatment. Unlike the presumption in U.S. jurisprudence, most other nations operate under domestic systems that permit the selective and discriminatory treatment of enterprises in their jurisdiction.

The use of chosen instruments, of approved and disapproved firms, and similar devices is normal rather than exceptional in most countries. A commitment by such countries to national treatment is no guarantee against systematic discrimination.

Besides, there are numerous instances in which the foreign-owned subsidiary bulks so large in the economy and occupies so unique a position that there is no norm by which to determine whether the enterprise is in fact receiving nondiscriminatory treatment. It would be hard to say, for instance, just what nondiscrimination meant if applied to Southern Peru Copper in Peru or to Aramco in Saudi Arabia.

Nevertheless, difficulties of this sort can be partially bridged. Minimal standards can be developed in treaty form and provision for appeal to some international authority can be developed. Here again, the odds are that the less developed countries would be exceedingly hesitant to enter into agreements of this sort. Once again, therefore, realism suggests that early advances in this field would probably have to be confined to the advanced countries.

Observe the relationship between this set of recommendations and those made earlier regarding international capital movements. In the disentangling of national jurisdictions, one could readily contemplate that the countries concerned would jointly agree not to impose any restraints on the export of capital for foreign direct investment, subject to the usual GATT-style caveats relating to balance-of-payment difficulties and national security. In addition, as part of the undertaking to extend equitable treatment to foreign-owned subsidiaries, countries would be committed not to discriminate against such subsidiaries in establishment rights. As a consequence, the freedom that multinational enterprises enjoyed in establishing new activities would probably exceed the present situation. Would this increased freedom reduce the tension associated with their operations; or would it add to that tension?

The Heart of the Problem

The question serves to remind us that some of the toughest problems still remain. A great deal of what concerns host governments, local elites, American labor, and others is the strength, suppleness, and flexibility of such multinational enterprises, at least as perceived by those that must negotiate with them. Tension from that source could be allayed at the margin by substantially better disclosure on the part of the multinational enterprises covering the whole of the operations. Indeed, the tax proposals made earlier have the incidental virtue of requiring such disclosure.

But disclosure provisions, experience suggests, can only do a little in allaying the tension. A second step, therefore, might well be to set up a procedure under which major locational decisions on the part of multinational enterprises, such as decisions to locate additional production facilities, might be subject to a process of challenge and review. Such a process could either be national or international in scope. This sort of approach would be of special interest to labor unions, of course, since it relates to their desire to stop "runaway plants."

From the viewpoint of many multinational enterprises, a proposal of this sort opens Pandora's box; it is important, therefore, to be clear at once on just what such a procedure would be expected to achieve. A review procedure would be destructive if it blocked multinational enterprises from proceeding with their plans where those plans were consistent with the achievement of increased efficiency. Proposed projects that could be blocked, therefore, would be those based upon government subsidies, government restrictions, or government threats. Decisions that could be traced to private cartel agreements or decisions based on the firm's ignorance of more attractive alternative opportunities might presumably also be prevented. But efforts simply to arrest change would be destructive; in any case, they would probably suffer the fate of King Canute.

Each of the possibilities suggested in these last few pages requires considerably more development and elaboration. None of them sits easily in the framework of our present thinking. The justification for proposing them at this time stems from two facts: from the fact that the multinational enterprise itself is a revolutionary institution that may in the end generate revolutionary responses; and from the further fact that the capacity for governments to accept change is so much greater than it was a few decades ago. Indeed, there is a considerable possibility that the multinational enterprise problem will find itself shortly merged in a very much larger issue: how advanced nations can live side by side in a world in which physical and cultural space is so rapidly shrinking. This issue involves not only the multinational enterprise but all forms of international movements, of goods, of capital, of people, and of ideas. It may be that in dealing with the overwhelming problems that are arising from forces such as these, the problem of the multinational enterprise will have been solved as well.

V. Summary

Multinational enterprises, as a rule, contribute to global welfare. But the distribution of the gains is not assured; some parties gain more substantially and more surely than others. Even when an interested party gains in economic terms, its sense of confronting a strong and supple party whose interests are sometimes adverse is psychically disconcerting.

The tension that multinational enterprises generate is

especially marked in less developed countries, partly because their presence eventually represents a challenge to elite groups. Government leaders and local industrialists that originally welcomed such enterprises as collaborators often come to see them as rivals. Intellectual leaders outside the local establishment see them as adversaries from the very first. Besides, multinational enterprises are often seen as a threat to local ideologies.

In the advanced countries, one source of the tension created by multinational enterprises can be traced to basic cultural differences. Countries such as Britain, which conduct their relations with large enterprises on a basis that has much in common with U.S. norms, are generally more relaxed about their presence than countries that conduct those relations on a fundamentally different basis, such as France and Japan.

Everywhere, however, the seeming strength and flexibility of the multinational enterprise gives it the appearance of a formidable adversary for those that must negotiate with it. This includes not only foreign interests but U.S. labor as well — and even, at times, the U.S. government. Multinational enterprises seem in a position to shift the national locus of their operations when they feel pressed, whereas government and labor are anchored to an unchanging piece of national real estate. Even if abstractly they see the flexibility of the enterprise as an eventual advantage to them, the short-run problem of dealing with the enterprise on a basis of seeming inequality is disturbing.

The problem takes on acute form for member states of regional free trade areas. The price that a member pays for refusing the entry of a multinational enterprise is magnified by the risk that other members of the area may welcome it. The fact that such enterprises are in an easy position to consider alternative locations in such areas adds to the sense of tension.

The tension is increased by the problem of overlapping jurisdictions. At least two sovereigns can exert their influence on a foreign-owned subsidiary. The U.S. government sometimes exercises the prerogative, especially in problems relating to trading-with-the-enemy, antitrust, and capital movements.

Governments respond to these tensions in many ways. Practically all, including the United States, limit the rights of foreign-owned enterprises to establish themselves in especially "sensitive" industries such as ordnance and radio broadcasting. Many go further, requiring local ownership for part of the equity and requiring commitments on the use of local credit, the use of local materials, and the development of a flow of exports.

These discriminatory practices are broadening very rapidly. They are affecting government procurement practices, government financial assistance, government research subsidies, and so on. The erstwhile objective of national treatment is badly impaired, despite treaty commitments to the contrary. Enterprises at times are even receiving contrary commands from different sovereigns, directed to the action of the same subsidiary.

Advanced countries are likely to be more willing than less developed countries to engage in cooperative action to sort out these problems. The current negotiations involving the broadening and deepening of the European Communities may seem a disturbing factor with regard to such cooperation in the short run; but those negotiations will also create opportunities for progress on that front from time to time, provided the U.S. government is in a position to seize the opportunities.

To clear the decks for such action, the United States should get rid of its capital export controls, preferably by stages over a brief period.

The case for United States negotiation of tariff concessions in return for capital entry privileges in foreign countries is a dubious one, and a program of that sort is not recommended.

The case for negotiation of a "fair conduct code" is less clear; but the gains from such a code are likely to be trivial.

In narrow economic terms, schemes that contemplate the eventual automatic divestiture of subsidiaries are more likely to be hurtful than helpful to host countries. But if they are aware of that fact and still are attracted by such schemes as a means of alleviating the psychic tensions, it is not in the U.S. interest to resist such schemes. Certain specified forms of such schemes, however, are to be preferred to others.

The U.S. government should initiate steps to alleviate the tension over tax questions. Two possibilities exist. One, consistent with the approach with bilateral tax treaties, contemplates the multilateral development of rules on such contentious subjects as transfer prices, debt-in-lieu-of-equity, and cost allocations between parent and subsidiary. Another, much more radical in approach, contemplates the formula allocation of global consolidated profits among the units that make up the multinational enterprise.

A group of interrelated and inseparable commitments are proposed to deal with the sensitive problem of overlapping national jurisdictions. These include: (1) the acceptance of self-denying ordinances by signatory states in certain stated fields, limiting their jurisdiction to the water's edge; (2) provision for the harmonization of national policies in these stated fields; (3) acceptance of the principle that foreign-owned subsidiaries will have certain guaranteed rights of operation, reducing the scope for systematic discrimination against them; and (4) an international organization for the enforcement of the interrelated commitments.

The toughest problem of all remains: how to reduce the sense of the negotiating parties that the multinational enterprise has superior opportunities for choice. A national or

international procedure is proposed for
cational decisions of multinational enterp
of directly affected parties. Only those l
that were based on "artificial" factors, su
subsidy or government threat, would be su

Future of the Multinational Enterprise

(Reprinted from *The International Corporation,*
edited by Charles P. Kindleberger © 1970,
Massachusetts Institute of Technology,
by permission of The M.I.T. Press)

Future of the Multinational Enterprise

In the field of social sciences, there is no such thing as being qualified to predict the future. Predictions of the behavior of social institutions are notoriously unreliable. The process whose outcome is to be predicted generally falls in that nasty category of human activity known as games between adversaries, not in the more manageable category of games against nature. Accordingly, one dare not make simple extrapolations based on historical relationships.

Still, wherever man shapes policy, he needs prediction on which to frame his policy. Let me launch this exercise by identifying the factors that I consider to be most critical in shaping that future.

Models for Projection

In order to deal with a phenomenon as complex and as heterogeneous as the multinational enterprise, one has to begin with some gross simplification; the peculiarities, idiosyncrasies, and irrationalities that are so important in explaining the individual actions of individual firms have to be set aside in a search for basic forces and tendencies. In brief, some kind of "model" of multinational enterprise behavior has to be constructed and tested as a basis for projection.

NOTE: This paper was financed by a grant from The Ford Foundation to the Harvard Business School.

After exposure to the available evidence, I find the relatively straightforward competitive model, with its emphasis on factor prices and factor endowments, to have only a limited utility as a basis for projection. The strength of multinational enterprise, such as it is, seems based on nonclassical factors such as proprietary knowledge and upon advantages of physical and organizational scale. Its motives for existence include profits, to be sure. But the path to profits is perceived as inseparable from absolute growth, and as involving a process of minimizing risk, offsetting threat, and hedging against uncertainty — all this in a setting in which the actors are few and fairly well identified. The first step in any projection, therefore, is to pin down the critical elements in the oligopolistic process that animate the multinational enterprise.

The role of the market

The evidence is reasonably clear that many enterprises have become "multinational" in order to penetrate or protect a market that they feared could not be served by exports.[1] The history of U.S. direct investment in foreign

---

[1] For the investment process within the investing firm, and the considerations that seem relevant in the process, see Y. Aharoni, *The Foreign Investment Decision Process* (Boston: Division of Research, Harvard Business School, 1966), especially Chaps. 3–7. For the results of other surveys on the motivation question in international investment, see R. S. Basi, *Determinants of United States Direct Investments in Foreign Countries* (Kent, Ohio: Kent State University Bureau of Economic and Business Research, 1963); A. N. Hakam, "The Motivation to Invest and the Locational Pattern of Foreign Private Industrial Development in Nigeria," *Economic and Social Studies*, Vol. 8, No. 1 (March 1966), p. 50; G. L. Reuber and F. Roseman, *The Takeover of Canadian Firms, 1945–1961: An Empirical Analysis*, Economic Council of Canada, Special Study No. 10 (Ottawa: Queen's Printer, 1969); National Industrial Conference Board, *U.S. Production Abroad and the Balance of Payments* (New York: NICB, 1966), p. 63; A. Stonehill and L. Nathanson, "Capital Budgeting and the Multinational Corporation," *California Management Review* (Winter 1967); R. F. Mikesell, ed., *Private and Government Investment Abroad* (Eugene, Oregon: University of Oregon,

markets, covering the full century during which such investments have been occurring, is rich with the evidence of the importance of that kind of factor. The process generally began with the acquisition by a U.S. enterprise of some sort of innovational lead — some technical or organizational skill, some production or marketing capability, that was not widely shared by others. United States businessmen have repeatedly developed markets in Canada, Britain, and Western Europe for manufactured goods, exporting products that were based on such a lead; then they have shifted their supply strategy to one based on production from an overseas subsidiary closer to these foreign markets.

The reasons for the shift were usually clear. At some point, the overseas markets of U.S. business grew large — sufficiently large so that much of the scale economies of production could be captured overseas. Where tariffs were imposed and where freight costs had any importance, that situation arose sooner than otherwise.

Besides, as the U.S. innovator's original lead began to be appropriated and imitated by others, the incentive of the innovator to consider whether average production costs in the overseas market might be lower than the marginal costs of output delivered from the United States began to take on a certain urgency. Where the specialized external economies of the U.S. environment did not seem to matter very much,

---

1962), p. 89; *Overseas Operation of U.S. Industrial Enterprises, 1960–1961* (New York: McGraw-Hill, 1960); National Planning Association, *Case Studies of U.S. Business Performance Abroad,* 11 case studies (Washington, D.C.: NPA, 1955–1961); H. J. Robinson, *The Motivation and Flow of Private Foreign Investment* (Menlo Park, California: Stanford Research Institute, 1961), Investment Series No. 4, p. 24; D. M. Phelps, *Migration of Industry to Latin America* (New York: McGraw-Hill, 1936), pp. 43–87; M. Kidron, *Foreign Investments in India* (London: Oxford University Press, 1965), pp. 253–256; B. L. Johns, "Private Overseas Investment in Australia: Profitability and Motivation," *Economic Record,* Vol. XLIII (June 1967), pp. 257–261; W. Winiata, "United States Managerial Investment in Japan," (unpublished Ph.D. thesis, University of Michigan, 1966), p. 110.

and where the ordinary mix of industrial labor skills available in most industrialized countries seemed sufficient for production purposes, the examination often led to a decision on the part of the U.S. businessman to invest in overseas production facilities.[2]

There have been cases, of course, in which the initial competitive edge that the businessman thought himself as possessing was one that could not be tested in the first instance by way of exports. In these cases, his decision to use his apparent competitive advantage as a basis for setting up an enterprise in a foreign country has generally involved more risk. Take, for instance, the foreign investment decisions of the food processing companies whose final product, such as green peas or margarine, seems unrelated to sophisticated skills and innovation. Companies of this sort have seen themselves as having a special capacity for mobilizing, financing, and directing the activities of independent farmers; for standardizing and controlling quality in the mass manufacture of tricky organic materials; and for controlling the distribution of perishable products in a way that reduced the threat of deterioration. Skills of this kind, where they exist, generally have to be exercised close to the market; the available choices for those who thought they possessed the skill was either to license a foreign producer, or to take the

---

[2] The sequence is described at much greater length in R. Vernon, "International Investment and International Trade in the Product Cycle," *Quarterly Journal of Economics*, Vol. LXXX (May 1966), p. 190. For a similar rationale, developed some years earlier, see S. H. Hymer, "The International Operations of National Firms," (unpublished Ph.D. thesis, M.I.T.); also C. P. Kindleberger, *American Business Abroad* (New Haven: Yale University Press, 1969), p. 11 *et seq.*; and B. Balassa, "American Direct Investments in the Common Market," *Banca Nazionale del Lavoro, Quarterly Review* No. 77 (June 1966), p. 134. The same kind of motivation for overseas direct investment by United Kingdom firms is suggested in J. H. Dunning, "Further Thoughts on Foreign Investment," *Moorgate and Wall Street* (Autumn 1966), p. 20.

investment plunge without previously testing the waters by way of exports.

Cases of this kind are to be found not only in the field of manufactured products but also in the sale of services. When skill in purveying services is involved, it is especially difficult to use the export route in order to test the marketability of what one has to offer. Here again, one usually has to test one's marketing advantage by setting up a subsidiary abroad. This is what lay behind the bold overseas expansion of U.S. life insurance companies in the 1880s, of U.S. banking organizations after World War I, and of U.S. hotels, supermarket companies, and management advisory services after World War II.

Investment decisions are, of course, usually the result of a complex amalgam of factors. Still, there is considerable evidence for the view that many investment decisions of multinational enterprises have been stimulated, not by the desire for bold initiatives aimed at exploiting some perceived advantage in organizational skill or technological information, but by a much more defensive consideration. The literature is rich in allusions to such defensive behavior in the oligopolistically structured industries where the bulk of such investment occurs.

The simplest case of a defensive investment is that of a U.S. industrial supplier who is invited by a major U.S. customer to follow the customer abroad in order to supply him at some foreign location. The subtle threat in a failure to follow such advice is generally not missed by the supplier.

But there are other variants in the defensive investment pattern. Picture a U.S. businessman in a carefully balanced domestic industry whose business horizon stops at the water's edge. Suddenly, one of his domestic rivals makes a move beyond his ken, setting up a local producing subsidiary in Turkey or Peru. For the U.S. firm that has not yet made a move, the problem is to determine the intent of the innovator. Can it be to preempt a market hitherto unknown to the laggard firm, one that will soon be perceived as highly attractive; or can it be to generate a new supply of the product, on a cost basis that can undercut U.S. sources? It is a complacent businessman who, lacking firsthand knowledge, can push such worries and uncertainties wholly out of his mind. And if our defensive businessman has little faith in any investigatory process for so large and uncertain a decision, if he believes principally in learning by doing where initial information is limited, then an obvious response is to match the investment move of his innovating rival.

Besides, imitation offers the best chance of leaving the oligopoly undisturbed. If both investors are right, an opportunity exists for the follower to share the innovator's benefits. If both prove wrong, there may be a problem of absorbing the cost of the error; but if the oligopoly is collectively strong, the cost of any error can be passed on. But if the innovator proves right and there is no imitation, then the oligopoly balance is imperiled.

In the occasional cases in which European parent enterprises have acquired U.S. subsidiaries, similar motivations sometimes seem to have played a role. Olivetti's well-publicized acquisition of Underwood in the United States was inspired by a desire to share with its U.S. rivals all the stimuli and challenges that the U.S. market was presumed to afford.[3] If U.S. firms were prodded and aided by their environment to generate new products and processes, so the argument went, then one could best protect one's self from

---

[3] Cases of the Harvard Business School, *Ing. C. Olivetti & Co. S.P.A.,* *(A–1 . . . A–6)* (1967). If Olivetti had been aware of the earlier Unilever example, that example would only have bolstered the company's convictions. As Unilever's historian sees it, Unilever's penetration of the U.S. market in the first half of the century was important principally for the stimulus it gave to the whole system's technical and marketing skills. C. Wilson, *Unilever, 1945–1965* (London: Cassell, 1968), pp. 228–236.

the rivalry of U.S. firms by being exposed to the same set of stimuli.[4]

Responses of this sort on the part of firms outside the United States have not been frequent, however. Perhaps a shortage of finance capital contributed to the infrequency of such responses. More likely, however, the problem for large European firms has been to identify the technological or organizational advantage that might serve as a basis for helping them survive the cold plunge into the large, competitive American environment. It is probably no coincidence that those that took the plunge generally did have some technological lead at the time of entry: Pechiney's American aluminum plant was one of the most advanced in the world; Olivetti had reason to believe that she brought real production strengths to her American subsidiary, not readily matched by her U.S. competitors. But the possession of a clear technological lead on the part of firms outside the United States is not all that common. And as long as this is so, the Olivetti-Pechiney kind of response will be slow in coming.

The search for raw materials

While the pursuit and protection of markets have been driving forces in the generation of multinational enterprises, the pursuit and protection of raw-material sources have been yet another. With their markets well secured, companies that once had relied upon domestic raw materials or upon foreign materials that others were producing, found themselves reaching abroad to control offshore raw-material sources.

---

[4] Pechiney's motives in acquiring an interest in Howmet in the United States, on the other hand, seem to have been based partly on the availability of cheap power for the production of aluminum, a motive that does not fit the pattern in the text. See "Pechiney Multinational," *Entreprise*, No. 679 (September 14, 1968).

The motives for such overseas investment were various. In reviewing those motives, one must not overlook such straightforward drives as a search for cheaper raw materials; nothing more complex than that seems to have sparked the early operations of the Braden and the Guggenheim interests in Chile and Mexico, for instance. But the motives explicitly articulated by the big overseas raw-material investors have often been more complex. What are these drives?

In a world in which the number of independent sources of raw-material supply is low, industrial processors of the material are uneasy about their likely treatment in times of shortage. If some of their suppliers are also rival processors, then the uneasiness takes a more acute form; for then the supplier is in a position, in times of shortage, to price his raw material at levels that would drive the processor out of business. The obvious response has been for the fabricator to search diligently for his own controlled sources of supply.[5] The consequence has been that international trade flows in highly concentrated industries such as copper, aluminum, lead, zinc, and bauxite, are dominated by the interaffiliate sales of international companies; and, further, that the geographical pattern of trade flows is better explained by the affiliate relationships of the buyer and seller companies than by any other measurable factor, such as distance.[6]

---

[5] For oil, see E. T. Penrose, *The Large International Firm in Developing Countries* (London: George Allen & Unwin, 1968), pp. 40–51, 150–172; and J. C. McLean and P. W. Haigh, *The Growth of Integrated Oil Companies* (Boston: Division of Research, Harvard Business School, 1954); for aluminum, Organization for Economic Cooperation and Development, *Gaps in Technology, Nonferrous Metals* (Paris; OECD, 1968), mimeo, pp. 38–47. More generally, E. T. Penrose, *The Theory of the Growth of the Firm* (Oxford: Basil Blackwell, 1968), p. 147.

[6] J. E. Tilton, "The Choice of Trading Partners: An Analysis of International Trade in Aluminum, Bauxite, Copper, Lead, Tin, and Zinc," *Yale Economic Essays*, Vol. VI (Fall 1966), p. 474.

The defensive response has gone further in certain respects. Raw-material exploitation is a chance affair from many different points of view. First, there is the risk of failing to find a producing mine or well. Then there is the risk of having the production blocked, whether by strikes, acts of God, or governmental interference. There is a strong incentive, therefore, for a firm to multiply the sources of its supply and to spread them geographically without strict regard for least-cost considerations.

The seeming downgrading of simple cost analysis is produced by still another factor, that of unpredictability. One cannot always say if North Sea gas, or Alaska and Nigerian offshore oil, or Peruvian copper is cheap or dear, at least not in time for the knowledge to be useful. Moreover, irrespective of the cost of the new source, one always has to guard against the possibility that it may be given privileged access to some major market. If others are plunging ahead, therefore, the risks of inaction may be very high.

Of course, the ultimate reaction in risk avoidance is for prospective rivals to pool their efforts in new high-risk areas. That pattern is to be observed in the many joint ventures among producer firms in the exploration and exploitation of crude oil and minerals.[7] This reaction reduces the possibility that any one of the producing rivals can have a very different experience from any of the others, whether in the

---

[7] A recent manifestation of some of these drives is British Petroleum's venture into Alaskan oil and the U.S. retail market; see, e.g., *The Economist* (March 8, 1969), p. 62. While the motivations of all parties to that venture were exceedingly complex, the force of the oligopolistic incentive balancing was apparent throughout the transaction. The Royal Dutch/Shell entry into North America decades ago represented still another variant of oligopolistic behavior. Reacting to Standard Oil's penetration of the Netherland Indies, Royal Dutch entered the United States, thus posing a threat to Standard if it misbehaved; see *The Royal Dutch Petroleum Company*, Diamond Jubilee Book, (The Hague, 1950), p. 16.

vagaries of prospecting or in the subsequent costs of operation.

Integration and scale

In response to stimuli of the sort just described, multinational enterprises have extended their reach, moving in an uninterrupted spread upward to their sources of raw material and downward toward their markets. As a result, there has been a remarkable increase in the number of overseas subsidiaries of U.S. parents over the past few decades. The growth is well documented in the case of a group of 187 such parents whose overseas activities have been traced back to 1900; this group of 187 probably accounts for over 80% of U.S.-foreign direct investments in manufacturing outside of Canada. At the end of World War I, the number of foreign subsidiaries in this group somewhat exceeded 250; by 1929, it had reached 500; by 1945, it was just under 1,000; by 1957, about 2,000; and by 1967, over 5,500.[8]

There is a good deal of persuasive evidence, albeit of an unstructured sort, that the nature of the multinational enterprises has tended to change during the process of spread. Recall how much stress was placed earlier upon the primacy of the U.S. market as the genesis of the dynamic forces that led to investment. In the case of the manufacturing enterprises, a firm-specific technology or firm-specific organizational skill provided the jumping off point for the U.S. parent into foreign markets. In the case of the raw-material producers, overseas investment was originally motivated in part by a concern to prevent prospective rivals from threatening the home market with the help of low-cost foreign supplies.

In the course of time, however, the process of vertical and horizontal spread has tended to place multinational enter-

---

[8] Some of the increase in numbers was probably the result of a conversion of branches to subsidiaries, but the factor was not important enough to account for the growth.

prises with U.S. parents in a global arena. It is true that the markets of the United States retain a dominant place inside these multinational structures. But the non-U.S. business of such systems has been growing far faster than their U.S. business. Along with this shift, the antennas that U.S. firms employ to scan their business environment have increased in reach and power. As a result, the major raw-material producers have come to think of themselves as operators of a global logistical system — carrying their product from wellheads or pitheads all over the world to markets equally dispersed, using any channel that makes business sense. The giant automobile companies have gradually taken a similar global approach. Their propensity for producing components in one country for assembly in a second and marketing in a third has grown enormously. The same can be said of firms producing components for standardized electronic products, such as radios and television sets.

One can, of course, overstate the importance of the global viewpoint among the multinational enterprises. The U.S. oil companies probably look upon their new oil discoveries on the Alaskan northern slopes with a special satisfaction, a satisfaction that a Canadian discovery would not quite impart. And the U.S. automobile companies' decision to produce the new 1970 compact car lines in the United States was probably induced by a set of calculations that was not entirely confined to comparisons of cost in rival locations; questions of relations with the U.S. government and U.S. labor unions were surely involved. Nevertheless, the relative weight of U.S.-based considerations has declined, even if the rank-order position of such considerations has not yet changed.

To speculate effectively about the future of multinational enterprises, one is obliged to confront the question whether such enterprises may be parlaying an initial advantage derived from some firm-specific capability, such as proprietary tech-

nology or access to a scarce raw material, into a more endur-
ing advantage based on the sheer size of the enterprise.
Need one assume that long after IBM's unique skill in the
production of third-generation computers has been disseminated to the world, IBM will retain its business advantage
on the basis of the sheer size it has meanwhile managed to
attain?

This is an extraordinarily complex question, one to be
approached with a certain diffidence. Multinational enterprises have almost certainly increased in relative prominence
over the past few decades. There is a certain amount of
evidence that U.S. firms engaged in multinational activities
have higher rates of growth, as well as a higher return on
capital, than do U.S. firms in similar industries which confine their activities to domestic markets.[9] There is also
some evidence that the foreign subsidiaries of multinational
enterprises have generally been growing faster and producing more efficiently than the local competition they confront in the overseas markets where they are located.[10] According to some back-of-the-envelope estimates, the business
of such enterprises outside their home countries may total
as much as $500 billions of goods and services, about one-
quarter of the gross product of the non-Communist world.[11]
Until one can look at the record of growth and profitability
by individual product lines rather than by industries, however, he feels unsure of the meaning of the data he confronts.

---

[9] This conclusion is based on an unpublished study by my colleague, Professor
Lawrence E. Fouraker.

[10] The data on growth rates are firmer than those on productivity. See D. T.
Brash, *American Investment in Australian Industry* (Cambridge, Mass.: Harvard University Press, 1966), pp. 27, 171; J. H. Dunning, *American Investment in British Manufacturing Industry* (London: George Allen & Unwin,
1958), passim.

[11] J. Polk, "The Economic Implications of the Multinational Corporation,"
U.S. Council, International Chamber of Commerce (February 14, 1969),
mimeo, p. 15.

At the present stage, one is reduced to armchair speculation concerning the nature of the competitive strengths that seem to be associated with multinational enterprises, speculation supported here and there by data and illustration. This sort of rumination suggests that the strength of multinational enterprises is usually based in the first instance on firm-specific capabilities. Multinational enterprises are identified with the development and application of new products and processes and with prolonging the proprietary advantages of such products and processes through adaptation and geographical spread. That advantage, in turn, seems to rest on a number of different types of scale advantage, including scale economies associated with the insurance principle, economies of the utmost importance in the innovating stage. There may be added economies that go with the establishment of a global information network that can efficiently accumulate knowledge regarding sources and markets. In any case, multinational enterprises are not identified with the manufacture of such standardized products as steel bars and rods, gray cloth, or plywood; but they are identified with products whose specifications are in flux. The dichotomy is not all that clear, of course. A few seemingly standardized products, such as automobiles, appear to enlarge their scale economies of production or distribution with such regularity and persistence that the advantages of the multinational enterprises are maintained. This may be part of the explanation for the international dominance of U.S. cigarette subsidiaries as well.

But if production and distribution scale economies cannot be counted on to grow constantly, one can see why the development of the multinational enterprise may be self-arresting. As the technology or organizational skill associated with a given line of manufactures is disseminated and appropriated by the world at large, the multinational enterprise may begin to lose any advantage based on its original proprietary lead in the affected line. If the demand for the product or service grows rapidly and if the optimum level of production or distribution for the individual firm grows more slowly, then the market may be able to accommodate more and more entrants. If multinationality entails overheads and inefficiencies not shared by its national rivals, the advantage may even be reversed.

There have been very few systematic tests of this semantical model, as far as I am aware.[12] Some industries, such as the copper industry and the petroleum industry, seem to be responding simultaneously to both the elements that strengthen the position of multinational enterprise and those that weaken it. In these industries, one can discern both a tendency toward more complete vertical integration on the part of existing firms and a tendency toward the introduction of new producers at the refining and exploiting stages.[13] With both tendencies occurring at the same time, it is unlikely that the usual measures of industry concentration and industry dispersion will help much to illuminate the trend.

One also sees some lines of manufacture, however, that appear to behave consistently with the hypothesis of self-arresting growth. The tendency is apparent, for instance, in nine major petrochemicals, whose industry structure has been traced from their genesis to their present state. In this case, the early dominance of multinational enterprises was rapidly eroded over the decades by the entry of national producers.[14] More impressionistically, one seems to see the

---

[12] A more detailed version of this model appears in an article by R. Vernon, "Organization as a Scale Factor in the Growth of Firms," in J. W. Markham and G. F. Papanek, eds., *Industrial Organization and Economic Development* (Boston: Houghton Mifflin Company, 1970).

[13] See the sources cited earlier in footnote 5.

[14] In these nine petrochemicals, 100% of the "initial" plants were those of multinational enterprises; but in the first following stage — a stage of very rapid growth — 59% of the additional plants established were those of multinational enterprises; in the second following stage, a period of slower growth, the comparable figure was 47%; and in the third following stage, one of

same tendencies in such relatively "mature" industries as metal industries, paper production, consumer electronics, and other consumer hardgoods. The conclusion to be drawn is trite, but significant: the scope of multinational enterprises depends in part on how rapidly technology is disseminated to national companies and assimilated by them.

The elements projected

If oligopolistic responses play as dominant a role in the behavior of multinational enterprises as this analysis suggests, then any projection of the future of such enterprises depends on how such enterprises define the geographical scope of their markets in the future. In industries where a basis for oligopoly exists, what is the scope of the geographical area that the principal participants will scan for opportunity and for threat?

Three or four decades ago, it was already clear that the main participants in some industries were beginning to think of their arena as global in scope. This was certainly true of the oil industry, of some of the nonferrous metals industries, and of certain branches of the chemical and machinery industries. But there was a wistful hope among the leading participants of these industries that uninhibited competition could be held in check. Large firms that had the competitive power to extend their reach to global markets were often prepared to forego that possibility if their prospective competitors in other countries would agree to limit their reach as well.

Until World War II, therefore, cartels were endemic in the industries characterized by high concentration and large firms; and one guiding principle of many of these cartels was to allocate markets on geographical lines to each of the

still slower growth, the figure was 35%. Adapted from R. B. Stobaugh, Jr., "The Product Life Cycle, U.S. Exports and International Investment" (unpublished D.B.A. thesis, Harvard Business School, 1968).

participants in the cartel.[15] Partly as a result, the process of
interpenetration by large firms in the markets of their rivals
in the period between the two world wars seems to have
slowed down. The activities of the overseas manufacturing
subsidiaries of U.S. firms grew only slowly up to World
War II; [16] and the spread of the Western Hemisphere subsidiaries of European firms, with the exception of a few
ebullient drug and machinery companies, also seems to have
been arrested.

In the years immediately following World War II, however, U.S. businessmen no longer seemed interested in maintaining a geographical division of world markets. European businesses, though slower on the whole to respond to
the change, also show signs of breaking out of their geographical shells. If the above arguments have any validity, then one
of the lines of response of the large European firms acting
to reduce the threat of their U.S. competitors and to reestablish oligopolistic equilibrium will be to accelerate their investments in the Western Hemisphere. One might then
picture the reestablishment of some sort of uneasy stability in
the highly concentrated industries, approximating the kind
of unspoken half-truce that is characteristic of such industries
in national markets.

But how important are we to assume that oligopolistically
structured industries will be in the future, especially those
industries in which multinational enterprises have exhibited
their greatest strength?

The rate at which businessmen attempt to develop new
products and processes is a key variable. If multinational

---

[15] For a summary of these developments, see my "Antitrust and International
Business," *Harvard Business Review*, Vol. 46 (September–October 1968) , p. 78.
[16] For our 187 multinational enterprises, for instance, the number of such
subsidiaries outside the Western Hemisphere at the outbreak of World War
II was under 600; by 1967, the comparable figure would rise to over 3,000.
The characteristic pattern of cartel agreements was to assign Western Hemisphere markets to U.S. participants.

enterprises do possess some advantage over others in developing and exploiting opportunities of this sort in their early proprietary stages, then the proportion of world business in the hands of such institutions should grow in periods of rapid change. The assumption that is fashionable at the moment is that such change is exponential in nature; but, like any such assumption, this is a projection based on not much more than casual extrapolation. Still, we can probably take it for granted that the rate will continue to be high for another decade or two if not longer.

The second kind of question is whether the advances of the future are likely to involve high developmental costs and prolonged developmental time schedules of the sort that offer very large firms a competitive advantage. Will the direction be such as to emphasize jumbo innovations like fourth-generation computers, new power plant technology, and new airframe advances; or is the stress to be on the development of products that are smaller and more manageable in risk terms, as in the field of optics, photography, and metallurgy? Insofar as one can discern a trend over the past few decades, the movement toward huge discrete innovational steps involving relatively large commitments on the part of the developing agent seems to have grown.[17] But it is not apparent how one can determine what should be expected in the future.

As one turns from the rate and form of innovation to future trends in transportation and communication, the basis

---

[17] Evidence on the magnitude of the effort associated with successful industrial innovation and development is beginning to accumulate; on the whole, the materials suggest that the time and money commitments involved in industrial innovations of any significance are depressingly large. See, for instance, R. R. Nelson, ed., *The Rate and Direction of Inventive Activity* (Princeton: Princeton University Press, 1962), pp. 279–358; IIT Research Institute, *Traces: Technology in Retrospect and Critical Events in Science*, Vol. 1 (IIT, 1968); E. Mansfield, *The Economics of Technological Change* (New York: W. W. Norton, 1968), pp. 99–133.

for projection seems somewhat more solid. Here, it is reasonably sure that the spectacular decline in costs and increase in efficiency which have been evidenced in the past century will continue. Air freight promises to grow at rates that will equal its past record of 20% or so in real terms, as larger and more economical equipment replaces the existing stock. Sea freight facilities will also increase in efficiency, even if at a less spectacular rate, as containerized sea shipments expand and specialized carriers continue to be developed. Improvement in the international transmission of sounds and images also can be expected to continue.

The implications of these changes for the growth of multinational enterprises are extraordinarily complex and subtle. Take the issue of communication improvement. We may be in for a period in which information is not only generated more quickly but also appropriated more quickly. Multinational enterprises may be in a position to build quickly new caches of firm-specific information, creating a basis for a competitive lead; but they may confront an environment in which that information will be appropriated and applied more rapidly by national companies. It is hard to say, on the basis of this factor alone, whether the multinational enterprises will strengthen their relative position or weaken it.

To the extent that enterprises manage to keep a proprietary hold on their technological and organizational resources, the basis for a tight oligopolistic structure may yet exist in some industries. In the foregoing it was observed that easier communication will widen the scanning frontier of enterprises in such industries so that the market with which they identify themselves and the competitors to which they respond will be more broadly dispersed than ever. The scanning of broader horizons, however, need not lead to more overseas direct investment; it may simply lead to more exports and imports on the part of enterprises, while they confine their actual investment to national markets. What can one say about the relative use of investment, rather than trade, as a means of penetrating overseas markets?

In the usual multiplant locational model, location is a function of the shape of the production cost curve plus transport costs. If production scale economies increase, the propensity to export from some central producing point will grow; and if transport costs decline, the tendency for centralizing production will grow stronger still. On the other hand, if aggregate demand increases, the optimum-sized plant may be found to serve a smaller area, so that more plants may be needed.

The usual model, however, carries us only a little way in the international context. In international investment, locational decisions are colored, even dominated, by other considerations: by a need to learn by doing, by a fear of the imposition of national trade barriers, and so on. The simple locational model is swamped by factors of this sort, and the basis for any solid projection evaporates.

Any predictive exercise concerning the future of the multinational enterprise entails either an extraordinarily complex model or a bold intuitive leap; and it is not evident on its face which is the superior course. My intuitive estimate is that multinational enterprises will maintain their prominence in the output of world goods and services, and may even enlarge their position somewhat in the next decade or so. Their prominence will be more evident in the advanced technological sectors and in the industries that are reliant on raw materials that are subject to oligopolistic control. Multinational enterprises will be less evident with respect to the more mature and standardized products. Indeed, mature industries that are now dominated by multinational enterprises, such as consumer electronics and cigarettes, could very well become more nationally oriented in their ownership and structure.

If guesses of this sort prove valid, they still suggest difficulties for multinational enterprise. According to my projection, such enterprises will seem to be controlling and preempting certain especially sensitive areas of economic activity: industries whose raw materials are sold in a well-controlled, oligopolistic market, and industries whose technology is under tight control. In short, multinational enterprises are likely to maintain their strength in those areas of economic activity to whose control national governments are most sensitive. That is why I anticipate the continuation, perhaps the heightening, of tension between the multinational enterprise and the nation-state.

Role of the State

Whether or not the multinational enterprise grows in importance relative to national industry, the propensity of such enterprise to establish itself in the more sensitive areas of national life is bound to evoke a defensive response on the part of sovereign states. The form and intensity of that response no doubt will vary from one country to the next, as it has in the past. Factors of a cultural, historical, and social sort will certainly affect the level of tolerance, as the cases of Canada and Belgium attest. That tolerance will also depend on the economic costs and benefits of the foreign investment as perceived by the people and the government in the host country. Despite those national differences, however, there are a number of general lines of response that one can envisage.

Limiting the right to do business

Many countries profess in principle to grant national treatment to foreign-owned business; but few apply the principle without substantial qualifications.[18]

---

[18] The principle, as V. Folsom observes, is founded on the biblical admonition, "One law shall be to him that is homeborn, and unto the stranger that

In the less developed countries, qualifications on the national treatment principle have always been of major importance. For various reasons, governments in most of these countries have developed the practice of negotiating with foreigners over the terms of their entry and of applying conditions they would not impose on domestic investors. This practice grew up originally partly because of the nature of foreigners' investments, rather than because of their foreign-ness. Many of these early investments involved raw materials, the title to which was vested in the state, so negotiation could hardly be avoided. Besides, the early foreign investors encountered no settled structure of domestic law relevant to the operation of their enterprises. Corporate tax law, labor law, and other statutory enactments necessary to define the relations between business and the state were lacking; the rights and obligations of such investors, therefore, had to be determined by contract. Finally, raw-material producers generally required physical control over extensive stretches of remote, underdeveloped territory. In those cases, there were added issues to be elucidated: questions of developing and controlling roads, ports, and power; questions of administering justice; and so on.[19]

Although the underdeveloped condition of many countries led them initially to apply a case-by-case approach to foreign investors' proposals, most of these countries retained that approach after the original reasons for it had disappeared. The practice of judging each case on its individual

---

sojourneth among you." (Exodus 12:4) ; see his "Rights and Duties of Foreign Investors Abroad," *The Rights and Duties of Foreign Private Investors* (New York: Matthew Bender, 1965) . The practice is mired in complex qualifications; see H. Walker, Jr., "Provisions on Companies in the United States Commercial Treaties," *American Journal of International Law*, Vol. 50, No. 2 (April 1965) , pp. 373–393.

[19] For a brief summary of problems and practices associated with such arrangements, see R. Vernon, "Long Run Trends in Concession Contracts," *Proceedings of the American Society of International Law*, Sixty-First Annual Meeting, Washington, D.C. (April 27–29, 1967) .

merits by that time was well fixed in administrative procedures. Besides, there were chronic balance-of-payment difficulties to deal with, providing a new reason for close control over any activity that might give rise to foreign transactions. In the administration of balance-of-payment regulations, distinctions in the treatment of foreign-owned enterprises inevitably developed.

If governments in the less developed countries had not applied a case-by-case approach to foreign investment, however, the foreigners would probably have insisted upon it. The Damoclesian character of balance-of-payment controls often led foreign investors to negotiate for some assurances on entry. Besides, the widespread tax-exempting powers in many countries for "new and necessary industries" or "pioneer industries" or industries located in backward regions tempted foreign investors into negotiation for such exemptions.

By the 1960s, however, the tendency to apply special conditions of entry for foreign-owned enterprises could be found not only in the less developed countries but in many countries that were well along in development.[20] Even in the United States, limitations of this sort — some of them of rather long standing — existed in a number of business activities. Foreign-owned corporations were limited in their right to do business in banking, and were excluded from doing business in public broadcasting, coastwise shipping, minerals exploitation on public lands, and a number of other activities.[21]

---

[20] For general surveys, see United Nations, *The Status of Permanent Sovereignty over Natural Wealth and Resources* (New York: United Nations, 1962) , pp. 7–62; National Industrial Conference Board, *Obstacles and Incentives to Private Foreign Investment, 1962–1964* (New York: NICB, 1966) ; S. Hymer, *National Policies Toward Multinational Corporations* (1969) , mimeo; U.S. Bureau of International Commerce, Department of Commerce, *Overseas Business Reports*, various dates and countries.

[21] D. F. Vagts, "United States of America's Treatment of Foreign Investment," *Rutgers Law Review*, Vol. 17, No. 2 (Winter 1963) , p. 74.

Other advanced countries were imposing similar limitations, varying in scope and effect. In France, for instance, foreign-owned oil companies had been limited in their refining and distribution activities since the late 1920s; [22] a systematic screening of all proposed foreign investments had been in effect since the early 1960s.[23] In the well-publicized case of Japan, all foreign direct investments have been under tight control for two decades; in the late 1960s, the only industries for which foreigners had unrestricted establishment rights were 15 or so sectors that foreigners could be counted on to avoid, such as brewing, ice manufacturing, cotton spinning, and steel.[24] Even Britain, despite its long tradition of maintaining a liberal regime on capital movements for non-residents, was quietly negotiating with major foreign investors over the terms of entry.

The results of the negotiations between investors and host governments are sometimes recorded in formal agreements, under which the foreign enterprise assumes various explicit commitments in the fields of finance, production, marketing, control, labor practices, or equity-sharing. In other cases, where the style of a nation's administration is such as to boggle at explicit agreements of this sort, "assurances" are required of the foreign investor — "assurances," for instance, that the enterprise will expand exports or production, will train local managers, and so on.[25]

In recent years, as the screening and conditioning of foreign investment have grown more widespread, the range of practices discriminating against foreign-owned enterprise seems to have widened as well. The use of "buy at home"

[22] J. H. McArthur and B. R. Scott, *Industrial Planning in France* (Boston: Division of Research, Harvard Business School, 1969).

[23] A. W. Johnstone, *United States Direct Investment in France: An Investigation of the French Charges* (Cambridge, Mass.: M.I.T. Press, 1965).

[24] Organization for Economic Cooperation and Development, *Liberalization of International Capital Movements — Japan* (Paris: OECD, 1968).

[25] J. H. Dunning, *The Role of American Investment in the British Economy,* PEP Broadsheet 507 (February 1969).

preferences, a long-established policy of government procurement agencies, has now been extended to "buy at home except from foreigners." The procurement officers of some governments are no longer content to screen their suppliers simply by determining whether they are producing locally; local ownership of the producing facilities also is a basis for preference. British government agencies give preference to the product of British-owned computer companies, French agencies to French-owned companies, and so on. Now that European governments are subsidizing research on a fairly broad scale, officials administering the subsidy programs are beginning to raise questions over the ownership of national corporations that apply for subsidy; otherwise, they fear that they may be financing IBM's research in fourth-generation computers. In countries where access to local capital markets is a licensed privilege, the same sort of ownership consideration is being taken into account.

My expectation is that, in the years just ahead, the criterion of ownership will figure even more in the treatment of enterprise than has been the case in the past, and that the tendency will exist both in the advanced and in the less developed countries. But it is important to make a distinction at this point between discriminatory forms and discriminatory effects. It is not at all clear that nations will actually be able effectively to increase their discrimination against such companies. Indeed, it is here that the nub of the problem can be said to lie. With different degrees of intensity, practically all countries feel that something has been lost if their national industries are not nationally owned; but most countries are also aware that at times more is lost by excluding the foreigner than by admitting him. As the years go on, if multinational enterprises increase somewhat in scope and power, it seems likely that nations will feel that both kinds of losses are growing — that the loss associated with a diminution of national ownership is growing, and that the loss that would be associated with terminating the trend is growing too. That, at least, seems a reasonable inference if the size of efficient units of technology, money, and markets continues to grow. As a result, the issue will be elevated from one of moderate importance in the affairs of nations to one that is rather more significant.

Of course, an uneasy equilibrium might conceivably emerge, an equilibrium sustained on the one hand by the need of national governments for the money, magic, or markets of the multinational enterprises, and, on the other hand, by the urge of multinational enterprises to expand their reach. But I am inclined to doubt that such an equilibrium can be long sustained. If transportation and communication are improving as rapidly as I have suggested, the urge of the more dynamic industries to integrate production and distribution facilities across national boundaries is likely to become more intense. To be sure, if new trade barriers appeared, such barriers could reduce international cross-hauling. But if trade barriers were to reappear widely among advanced countries — an unlikely phenomenon — this would affect only the placement and function of subsidiaries, not their establishment. The other rewards and advantages of a multinational strategy, including the advantages that go with the interaffiliate transmission of technology and money, still would be present. The conflict between a global strategy on the part of multinational enterprises and a desire to retain national control on the part of the governments will be heightened. From time to time, in a spasm of frustration, there will be repressive acts on the part of individual states. How then will the multinational enterprises respond to this heightened state of tension?

Reaction to tension

The first instinct of multinational enterprises, we can be sure, will be to deal with the intrusions of governmental bodies on their own, without trying to elevate their problems to an intergovernmental issue.

The reaction is understandable enough. So far, multinational enterprises have displayed a remarkable capability for surviving in an environment of uncertainty and risk. Their confidence in their ability to deal with governmental hostility in the future is high. They are aware that trying to pit government against government may have a price, in terms of ill will and retaliation; and even when pressure is exercised by so powerful an advocate as the U.S. government, one cannot be sure it will work.

Of course, there is always the possibility that multinational enterprises might urge governments to develop some kind of agreed international order that would ease their lot. But even that kind of initiative has its dangers. Although a more elaborate international order conceivably could increase the predictability of the environment in which such enterprises operate, it would be hard to picture such a regime that did not at the same time reduce their flexibility of response. Accordingly, when multinational enterprises begin to feel the breath of governments at their backs, the disposition is to find some formula that relieves the pressure locally without widening the role of government. "Codes of fair conduct," "sharing ownership with local interests," and similar formulas are generally advanced. Actions that involve intergovernmental threat or intergovernmental collaboration take a very low place in the list of possible responses.

Not all intergovernmental measures are ruled out, however. Enterprises concerned with international business have been known to support limited and selective intergovernmental agreements where they feel such agreements would be helpful. After all, the International Convention for the Protection of Industrial Property — a convention safeguarding the rights of inventors and their assignees to secure patent protection in foreign countries — has been operating for

85 years or so; similarly with protective clauses in the field of trademarks. Bilateral treaties of establishment — sometimes dubbed "treaties of friendship, commerce, and navigation" in their more archaic form — have been negotiated between pairs of nations for many years; and bilateral treaties for the avoidance of double taxation have been sponsored by business interests where needed. But if U.S. enterprises looked charily on the uninhibited extension of such intergovernmental regimes, they would not be exhibiting an obvious kind of irrationality.

One is led to assume that if some more elaborate international regime should eventually emerge, it will not be because foreign investors were clamoring for it. More likely, it would arise out of a recognition on the part of governments that for one reason or another their interests demanded such a regime. That development could come about eventually if governments — particularly the U.S. government — began to distinguish their national interests from the interests of their multinational enterprises rather more explicitly than they have in the past. The possibility that this divergence of interest may occur is somewhat increased by the trend toward the multinationalizing of business; that is, by the increase in the relative importance of the "foreign" element in the total business of multinational enterprises. The growth in that element of the business increases the frequency of incidents in which the sovereign's capacity to enforce some national policy — such as a national monetary policy, a national antitrust policy, a national trading-with-the-enemy policy, or a national employment policy — seems to have been weakened. The realization that there are problems in this regard is nothing new; the question is whether the problems will grow.

That there will be some increase in such problems seems plausible in its face. For numerous reasons, multinational enterprises are not easily subjected to national policy. The

problem appears not only in a form that is familiar to host
countries, that is, in the context of applying national policies
to foreign-owned enterprises; it appears also in a form that
applies especially to the capital-exporting country. The
home government, when deliberating whether to apply its
jurisdictional power to the full, is obliged to consider the
reactions of other governments. For fear of offending other
governments, for instance, the United States finds itself
obliged to move judiciously and with circumspection when
it applies national regulations that might bear on the behavior of overseas subsidiaries. Problems have arisen in the
application of its trading-with-the-enemy regulations, the institution of its antitrust suits, the imposition of controls on
its direct investment flows, and so on.

Besides, there is a possibility that the issue could become
more symmetrical. Until recently, the United States has not
seriously had to confront the implications of the fact that
France may be in a position to influence the business policies
of Pechiney's U.S. subsidiary in the U.S. market. Heretofore,
the shoe has been on the other foot; accordingly, the United
States had tended to belittle the problem, as indeed it de-
serves to be belittled when gauged in pragmatic terms. But
if some of the highly concentrated manufacturing industries
should become more international in their structure, then
the United States may begin to develop some of the reactions
heretofore associated with host countries.

If the United States should develop those reactions, the
possibility of concerted response by nations will be somewhat greater than it appears at present. But what kind of
response is likely to be generated? Here, one strays beyond
the limits of projection into that of almost pure speculation.
But perhaps a little speculation is justified.

What nations shortly will discover when they turn to a
concerted approach is that the heart of the problem is its
least tractable part: how to ensure that the fruits of such

enterprises' operations are distributed among such nations in some "equitable" way. No one is likely to need much persuading that a tight case-by-case regulatory approach would be impossible in practice and very likely destructive in outcome. The principles of any negotiation, if not their implementation, will probably have to be comparatively simple; and, being simple, they may well have to allow some of the more vital problems posed by the multinational enterprise to go by the board.

One area in which some relatively arbitrary and simple principles could probably be negotiated is in the field of taxation. The progress that has been already achieved in the negotiation of bilateral agreements paves the way for the extension and multilateralization of tax arrangements. Besides, this is a field in which multinational enterprises themselves may see some advantages in pressing for the negotiation of agreements; this would be especially true if national taxing authorities, through increasing sophistication, managed progressively to reduce the value to these enterprises of their present flexibility. That flexibility depends partly on the inefficiency and limited competence of these authorities. As the company's discretion in areas like international transfer pricing, overhead allocation, debt in lieu of equity, and other familiar areas of accounting choice are reduced by more aggressive action on the part of national tax authorities, the firms themselves may perceive advantages in greater international tax collaboration. The approach to collaboration would presumably require the nations concerned to look upon intimately related affiliates as if they were a single enterprise. The problem would then be to define and allocate the profit of the enterprise irrespective of where that profit might nominally appear.

Another area that lends itself to international collaborative effort is the avoidance of clashes between sovereign states arising out of their joint jurisdiction over subsidiaries.[26] In this area, one could picture a set of agreements based on several interrelated principles.

The first principle would be that, with regard to certain areas of national policy, no government would try to influence the overseas subsidiaries of its national companies by coercion of the parent. An agreement of this sort, if multilateral in scope, would be confined to nations that saw something to be gained in a reciprocal commitment; and it would be confined to subjects in which the self-imposed restraint did not raise the specter of significant injury to the participating countries. One could picture, for instance, agreements of this sort among the advanced countries, covering activities in the fields of antitrust, trading with the enemy, corporate disclosure, corporate financing, and so on. Since such agreements might ease the lot of the multinational enterprises themselves, it is even possible to envisage eventual support from that quarter.

A second principle emerges as a natural corollary of the possibility just mentioned. This is the revitalization through international treaty of the principle of national treatment for foreign nations — but a revitalization accompanied by the rehabilitation of the Calvo Clause; that clause, it will be recalled, would deny all domestic rights and remedies to any foreign-owned subsidiary if it invokes the diplomatic support of a foreign government (for which read "the United States") in a dispute with its host government.

Each of the two principles so far suggested requires some kind of international adjudicating mechanism in order to be operative. Countries are bound to be accused of violations from time to time. Besides, no responsible country could withdraw its protective shield from the overseas subsidiaries

---

[26] The word "subsidiaries" is used loosely here. The same points may well apply to other types of entity located abroad that have a jurisdictional personality in the host country, even if technically they were branches.

of its nationals unless it left behind some set of credible safeguards which might take the place of that shield.

An approach of this sort would have a somewhat greater chance of being launched among the advanced countries alone than on a global basis. For one thing, most U.S. parent firms, being understandably disposed to the avoidance of the untried, would probably prefer to limit any innovation of this sort to the comparative safety and security of the advanced countries' jurisdictions. Moreover, many of the less developed countries would probably resist any proposal that assigned an important role to international adjudication, fearing the internal domination of the advanced countries in any intergovernmental tribunal.

The probability that this approach would be confined to the advanced world is enhanced by another major factor. Nations involved in any agreements that relinquished their hold on overseas subsidiaries would probably wish to protect themselves from the risks that the subsidiaries' new-found freedom would imperil some important national objective. Accordingly, there might well be a need for a joint commitment on the part of the countries concerned to launch on a continuous, nonstop process of policy harmonization in the fields in which they were accepting restraints upon their exercise of sovereign power. One would not expect that the harmonization process would lead to identical national policies in these fields. In the business of trade with the Communist bloc, for instance, the present differences in national levels of control are probably quite tolerable. In the field of antitrust, on the other hand, other governments might have to be persuaded to exert some kind of control over agreements likely to be harmful to the other governments concerned; this might mean, for instance, persuading various countries to extend their anticartel legislation to export cartels, which usually are exempted from national antitrust laws. In short, where large differences existed and where these were perceived as generating major risks for any of the countries concerned, one could surely hope to find eventually the means of reducing these risks.

If all these things were done, however, some of the most difficult aspects of the operations of multinational enterprises — difficult in the sense that they challenge the control of member states in their own economies — would still lie outside the reach of these agreements. For instance, national employment policy and national monetary policy would still be subject to the actions of the multinational enterprises to a degree that might prove intolerable for the nations concerned.

One way to "solve" a difficult problem is to submerge it into an even larger one. In this case, the larger problem is already waiting in the wings. The threat to national policies will be mounting from many different directions: not alone from the existence of the multinational enterprise, but also from the shrinkage of trade barriers, the improvement in transport and communication, and so on. These are likely to raise issues of sovereignty that may, in the end, dwarf the multinational enterprise problem. Perhaps when that occurs, the resulting institutional adjustments will deal with the multinational enterprise as well.

Other DIVISION OF RESEARCH Books on
Multinational Enterprise

THE PRODUCT LIFE CYCLE AND INTERNATIONAL TRADE
LOUIS T. WELLS, JR., EDITOR

In recent years the theory of international trade has seen some dramatic innovations. The innovations have come largely as a result of what has appeared to be the inability of traditional theory to explain what has been observed in the real world. The traditional wisdom, classical and neoclassical trade theory, has been found by many to be inadequate to explain satisfactorily the actual flows of goods from one nation to another. The predictable result has been the generation of alternative hypotheses to explain the real world phenomena. One set of these hypotheses, generally called a "product life cycle model," has been found by a number of researchers to be useful in explaining flows of trade. Some of the tests of this model have been published; others have not previously been available. The papers in this book have therefore been brought together for two purposes: (1) to encourage the authors of the unpublished studies to make their findings available to a wider audience, and (2) to bring together in one volume the results of some of the important research.

(LC 78–184791, ISBN 0–87584–095–7, 1972, $3.00)

THE MAKING OF MULTINATIONAL ENTERPRISE:
A Sourcebook of Tables Based on a Study of 187 Major U.S. Manufacturing Corporations
JAMES W. VAUPEL AND JOAN P. CURHAN

As an outgrowth of the Harvard Business School's Multinational Enterprise Study under the direction of Professor Raymond Vernon, this book contains more than 500 tables based on data selected from the master data bank. These tables map the expansion and development of the foreign operations of the 187 corporations in the study from 1900 to 1967.

In a field where little data are available, this particularly extensive compilation should be of great interest to researchers and managers of multinational enterprise.

(LC 70–94408, ISBN 0–87584–081–7, 1969, $20.00)